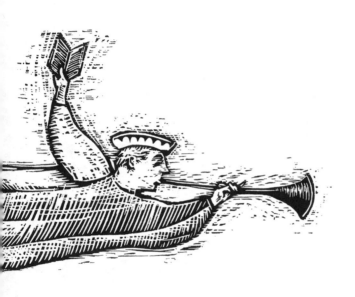

Mormon: *a brief theological introduction*

This publication was made possible by generous support from the Laura F. Willes Center for Book of Mormon Studies, part of the Neal A. Maxwell Institute for Religious Scholarship at Brigham Young University.

Published by the Neal A. Maxwell Institute for Religious Scholarship, Brigham Young University, Provo, Utah. The copyright for the 2013 text of The Book of Mormon is held by The Church of Jesus Christ of Latter-day Saints, Salt Lake City, Utah; that text is quoted throughout and used by permission.

Printed in the United States of America

ISBN: 978-0-8425-0014-2

LIBRARY OF CONGRESS CONTROL NUMBER: 2020902550

Mormon

a brief theological introduction

BRIGHAM YOUNG UNIVERSITY

NEAL A. MAXWELL INSTITUTE

PROVO, UTAH

Adam S. Miller

The Book of Mormon: brief theological introductions series seeks Christ in scripture by combining intellectual rigor and the disciple's yearning for holiness. It answers Elder Neal A. Maxwell's call to explore the book's "divine architecture": "There is so much more in the Book of Mormon than we have yet discovered. The book's divine architecture and rich furnishings will increasingly unfold to our view, further qualifying it as '*a marvelous work and a wonder.*' (Isaiah 29:14) . . . All the rooms in this mansion need to be explored, whether by valued traditional scholars or by those at the cutting edge. Each plays a role, and one LDS scholar cannot say to the other, '*I have no need of thee.*'"[1] (1 Corinthians 12:21)

For some time, faithful scholars have explored the book's textual history, reception, historicity, literary quality, and more. This series focuses particularly on theology—the scholarly practice of exploring a scriptural text's implications and its lens on God's work in the world. Series volumes invite Latter-day Saints to discover additional dimensions of this treasured text but leave to prophets and apostles their unique role of declaring its definitive official doctrines. In this case, theology, as opposed to authoritative doctrine, relates to the original sense of the term as, literally, reasoned "God talk." The word also designates a well-developed academic field, but it is the more general sense of the term that most often applies here. By engaging each scriptural book's theology on its own terms, this series explores the spiritual and intellectual force of the ideas appearing in the Latter-day Saints' "keystone" scripture.

Series authors and editors possess specialized professional training that informs their work but, significantly, each takes Christ as theology's proper end because he is the proper end of all scripture and all reflection on it. We, too, "talk of Christ, we rejoice in Christ, we preach of Christ...that our children may know to what source they may look for a remission of their sins" (2 Nephi 25:26). Moreover, while experts in the modern disciplines of philosophy, theology, literature, and history, series authors and editors also work explicitly within the context of personal and institutional commitments both to Christian discipleship and to The Church of Jesus Christ of Latter-day Saints. These volumes are not official Church publications but can be best understood in light of these deep commitments. And because we acknowledge that scripture demands far more than intellectual experimentation, we call readers' attention to the processes of conversion and sanctification at play on virtually every scriptural page.

Individual series authors offer unique approaches but, taken together, they model a joint invitation to readers to engage scripture in their own way. No single approach to theology or scriptural interpretation commands preeminence in these volumes. No volume pretends to be the final word on theological reflection for its part of the Book of Mormon. Varied perspectives and methodologies are evident throughout. This is intentional. In addition, though we recognize love for the Book of Mormon is a "given" for most Latter-day Saint readers, we also share the conviction that, like the gospel of Jesus Christ itself, the Book of Mormon is inexhaustible.[2] These volumes invite readers to slow down and read scripture more thoughtfully and transformatively. Elder Maxwell cautioned against reading the Book of Mormon as "hurried tourists" who scarcely venture beyond "the entry hall."[3] To that end, we dedicate this series to his apostolic conviction that there is always more to learn from the Book of Mormon and much to be gained from our faithful search for Christ in its pages.

—The Editors

Contents

Introduction

"The art of losing isn't hard to master."
—Elizabeth Bishop

Mormon is a terrifying book. It is a book about time, about the costs of time, and about what happens when we run out of time.

Mormon is a book about a man who lives through the end of the world. He loses everything and everyone he loves. His world collapses around him—socially, politically, economically, ecologically, religiously. He's forced to watch as his people's cities are destroyed, as their lands are burned, as their women and children are sacrificed to idols, and as hundreds of thousands of corpses pile up. Mormon, with his eyes wide open, "sees all life and stuff about him involved in a huge ceaseless combustion, a literal and apparent process of oxidation which is turning some things slowly, some rapidly, but all things surely to ashes."[1]

what can we learn from Mormon's experience?
As a theologian, I intend to read Mormon's book as a beginner's guide to the end of the world. I intend to read it as a case study in apocalyptic discipleship. My basic question is this: what does Christian discipleship look like when you are not just waiting for the end of the world but actually living *through* it?

My wager is that Mormon's apocalyptic discipleship can bring more clearly into view the underlying structure of discipleship itself. In particular, I'm betting on the following thesis: that living through the end of the world (on any number of scales) is *the* fundamental framework for Christian discipleship of any kind—by anyone, in any world, in any age.

To help bring this into focus, imagine some combination of the following scenarios.

Imagine, on the one hand, a certain kind of religion. Imagine a religion that required you to lose your life to save it (cf. Matthew 10:39). Imagine a religion whose introductory ritual required you to symbolically die, be buried, and then rise from the grave, committed now to living what remained of your life as something that belonged not to you but to God—bearing his name, filled with his Spirit, acting as his agent (cf. Romans 6:3–7). Imagine a religion that might, at any time, ask you, as Jesus did the rich young man, to "sell all that thou hast, and distribute unto the poor" (Luke 18:22). Imagine a religion premised on the necessity of sacrificing all things, a religion that claimed up front, as the Lectures on Faith do, that any "religion that does not require the sacrifice of all things, never has power sufficient to produce the faith necessary unto life and salvation" (Lectures on Faith, 6:7). Or imagine, finally, a religion that explicitly required you to return to God, by way of consecration, all of your time, talents, and possessions.

Can you imagine this sort of religion?

Can you imagine a religion that *required* the sacrifice of all things?

Now imagine, on the other hand, a certain kind of world. Imagine a world structured by time and pinned to its relentless flow. Imagine a world where everything that arises will also pass away, a world where, as Joseph Smith claimed, "as the Lord liveth, if it had a beginning, it will have an end."[2] Imagine a world where possessions decay, buildings crumble, triumphs fade, governments collapse, continents drift, and mass extinctions happen again and again.

Imagine a world where children grow up and leave home, where people get sick and grow old, where everyone dies. Imagine a world where the people you love—for as long as they live, for better or worse—are constantly changing. In this kind of world, people are more like rivers than rocks. They persist but never stay the same.

Imagine this kind of marriage, this kind of family, this kind of home. This isn't hard to do. My grandparents are dead. My father can no longer walk. The young man my wife married is gone forever. Our daughter is already grown and the five-year-old girl I held in my lap is never coming back. The sixteen-year-old girl I took to the movies is never coming back. Does this perpetual passing away hurt? Shouldn't it? Resurrection doesn't solve this problem. Immortality doesn't solve this problem. Resurrection doesn't freeze the world in place, trapping us in a block of ice-cold perfection. Resurrection is the promise that, in Christ, life can *continue* to pass, not that it will finally stop passing.

Imagine, then, a world where you are guaranteed to lose everything and everyone. Imagine a world where it is always possible to care for things but never possible to keep them.

Now, to press home the urgent, contemporary reality of such a world—and, perhaps, the urgent contemporary relevance of the Book of Mormon—take what we've imagined thus far and push it a step farther.

Imagine that these are actually the latter days. Imagine that the world itself is going to end, that "the earth shall be rolled together as a scroll, and the elements shall melt with fervent heat" (Mormon 9:2). Imagine a world that could end tomorrow in nuclear winter, in a cloudburst of ballistic missiles and blast

4

radii and poisonous fallout. Or imagine one single bomb that, all by itself, would be powerful enough to ruin the world and render it uninhabitable. Imagine that bomb going off instantaneously. Now imagine that bomb's detonation requiring a five-minute countdown, a twenty-four-hour countdown, a monthlong countdown, a yearlong countdown. Imagine, even, a world-ending bomb with a fuse the length of an average human life—when the baby is born, the fuse is lit—a fuse long enough for there "to be great doubtings and disputations among the people, notwithstanding so many signs had been given" (3 Nephi 8:4).

Regardless of how the world ends, we can rest assured that it is going to end. And regardless of how we lose everything and everyone we love, we *will* lose them—if only by the most quiet, familiar, and local means. Slowly and singly or swiftly and collectively, death will claim every one of us. "A person's life is like grass. Like a flower in the field it flourishes, but when the hot wind blows, it disappears, and one can no longer even spot the place where it once grew" (Psalms 103:15–16, NET).

Time will dispossess us all.

Now, recall the point of my asking you to imagine these troubling things. My thesis, as I indicated before, is that a life of Christian discipleship sits squarely at the crossroads of just this sort of religion and just this sort of world. Discipleship happens at the intersection of the requirement that we sacrifice all things and the inevitability of losing all things. As a result, to imagine a life of Christian discipleship you need only imagine a religion that requires you to sacrifice everything in a world that will, regardless, exact the loss of everything. Imagine, then, treading the path of discipleship and preemptively *willing*—as an act of love and sacrifice—your own already inevitable loss of all things. Imagine the practice of your religion as the business of willing the end of the world.

What would it look like to willingly give up your life and loved ones and world? What would it look like to give them up and *then* keep loving them and living with them and caring for them? What would it look like to sacrifice "all things" intentionally rather than just inevitably? How would it change your relationship to life? How would it change your relationship to property? How would it change your relationship to your parents, your spouse, your children? And how, in particular, would this sacrificial gesture utterly transform your relationship to time?

What would it look like to be a disciple of Christ as the world collapses around you?

What does discipleship look like at the end of the world?

It looks, I think, like Mormon.

1

A Note on the Practice of Theology

"All honest theology must be conducted 'within earshot of the dying Christ.'" —*Christian Wiman*

Theology can be practiced in any number of ways. In contemporary scholarship, systematic theologies, comparative theologies, and histories of theology tend to dominate. For my part, I practice theology as a form of "Christophysics." Taking Christ as theology's explicit end, I practice theology not as a form of history (what *did* religious people believe, say, or do?) or as a form of official dogmatics (what *should* religious people believe, say, or do?) but as a direct investigation into the fundamental forces at play in redemption. From what suffering and troubles does Christ rescue us and by what means is this rescue accomplished? What forces shape the need for and enable the realization of redemption? The urgent question at the heart of my work is always the same: exactly how, in Christ, are we saved?

Working as a Christophysicist, I primarily bring two sets of philosophical tools to bear. Grounding my theological work in scripture—in this case, primarily in the nine chapters of Mormon's book—my initial approach is hermeneutic. Hermeneutics is the work of offering very close and very careful readings of a received text. In other words, in order to generate the raw materials needed for further reflection, I begin by paying very close attention to Mormon's choice of words, to the contexts that accompany those choices, to the texts that he cites, to the themes that he emphasizes, to the history he assumes, to how he positions his readers, to the order in which he tells his story, to the underlying logic that guides his selection of what to include (or not) as part of that story, and—especially—to the larger constellations of meaning that emerge from the combination of these different elements.

Secondly, my approach is phenomenological. Phenomenology is a branch of philosophy that, rather than trying to get *behind* our lived experiences of the world to their historical, biological, or material roots, takes seriously what is given in the lived experiences themselves. As a theological tool, I use a phenomenological approach to investigate the nature of the lived experiences revealed in scripture. What kind of world emerges from the text? What kind of structure does this world have, with what is this world populated, and what forms of life unfold in response to it? In particular, what kinds of fundamental problems (like sin, death, and suffering) structure this world and what kind of redemption is possible in relation to them?

The details gathered in my close reading of the text are used both to fill out a picture of this world and to tie that picture as tightly as possible to the shared reality of our ordinary human experiences. In this way, my approach to theology is not *about* history or doctrines. Rather, my aim is to clarify the lived experiences that these histories and doctrines are *themselves* about. For me, histories and doctrines are not the goal. They are the raw material. When we insist that historical questions must always take priority over theological questions, we risk insisting that Christ can only be approached as an artifact. We risk privileging a husk of godliness while denying the power thereof (cf. 2 Timothy 3:5). We risk handcuffing Christ to the thin and fundamentally secular horizons of what can be historically verified. We risk, in short, bracketing Christ.

To paraphrase Ralph Waldo Emerson, my approach to theology prioritizes the working assumption that God not only was but *is*, and that he not only spake but *speaks*.[1] And, so, my interest in histories and doctrines will be supervened by the job of extracting from these raw materials a profile that brings Christ into sharp focus as a live power. Instead of being comprehensive or systematic, my work will be targeted and pragmatic. Instead of working in the past tense, I will work in the present tense. I will return to the same fundamental question again and again. How, in the details of this text, is the ongoing reality of Christ's redemptive power confirmed and revealed?

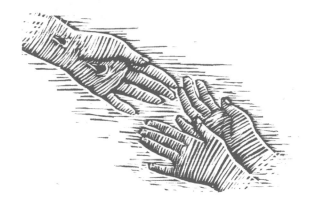

2

A Structural Synopsis

*"Your voice shall come from the ground like the voice of
a ghost, and your speech shall whisper out of the dust."*
—Isaiah 29:4, NRSV

Consider first the text of Mormon itself. While the
Book of Mormon is, as a whole, largely the product of
Mormon's ordering, summary, and abridgement, my
work here is focused (with an occasional nod to the
single chapter that composes the Words of Mormon)
on investigating the nine chapters that compose
Mormon's own contribution to that larger project.
What choices define Mormon's contribution? What
goals shape its composition? Introducing his own
record, Mormon tells us: "I, Mormon, make a record
of the things which I have both seen and heard, and
call it the Book of Mormon" (Mormon 1:1). On my
account, this is the essential thing to know about the
text of Mormon itself: Mormon not only *lived* as a witness, he shaped his book to *function* as a witness. Both
his life and his discipleship are defined by the work
of witnessing. He witnesses the world's passing away.
He witnesses violence and loss. He witnesses suffering
and death. And, through it all, he never stops witnessing that—nonetheless—Christ "hath gained the victory
over the grave" and "in him is the sting of death swallowed up" (Mormon 7:5).

With respect to the structure of the Book of
Mormon as a whole, Mormon's witness brings the

volume's central narrative history to its conclusion. That history, heavily accented by Mormon's overriding interest not in history itself but in the "things of God" (cf. 1 Nephi 6:3), focuses on "the record of the people of Nephi, and also of the Lamanites" (Title Page of the Book of Mormon). As we have it (minus the Book of Lehi), this history begins with the departure of Lehi's Israelite family from Jerusalem circa 600 BC, winds through the story of Lehi's descendants in the Americas and their fracturing into two warring parties, culminates with the appearance of Jesus Christ to the Nephites and Lamanites shortly after his resurrection, and concludes, circa 400 AD, with the implosion of the Nephites in a perfect storm of war, secret combinations, and open rebellion against God. Mormon's own story is intertwined with the horrifying details of this final implosion as he is forced to "witness the entire destruction of [his] people" (Words of Mormon 1:2).

Mormon's book, then, concludes the Book of Mormon's central narrative. What begins in 1 Nephi concludes in Mormon. With respect to that central narrative, the remaining two books contributed by Mormon's son Moroni constitute a kind of coda that recapitulates in miniature the arc of the Nephites' self-destruction with an abridged history of the Jaredites (the Book of Ether) and ties up loose ends with Moroni's own grab bag of final reflections (the Book of Moroni). If Mormon's book concludes the central narrative of the Book of Mormon by laying the Nephites to rest in a shallow grave of their own making, Moroni's contributions add a final, solemn headstone to that grave.

Mormon's own nine-chapter book mirrors the structure of the Book of Mormon on a smaller scale. It, too, is largely composed by Mormon with an addendum added by Moroni. In our current edition, Mormon consists of nine chapters. In the first seven chapters, Mormon recounts the end of his world. In the final two chapters, Moroni adds his own epilogue to his father's account. This split authorship breaks the book into its two primary pieces: chapters 1–7 as composed by Mormon and chapters 8–9 as composed by Moroni (See FIGURE 1, next page).

With respect to the structure of Mormon's contributions in chapters 1–7, it is also worth noting that our contemporary chapter breaks do not parallel the original 1830 chapter breaks dictated by Joseph Smith. The 1830 edition of the Book of Mormon used longer, unnumbered paragraphs instead of verses and, rather than dividing the text into nine chapters, divided it into four. The first chapter of the 1830 edition corresponds to chapters 1–3 of the current edition. The second chapter of the 1830 edition corresponds to chapters 4–5 of the current edition. The third chapter corresponds to chapters 6–7 and the fourth to chapters 8–9. Divided along these lines, the first three chapters of the 1830 edition were written by Mormon and only the fourth and final chapter was written by Moroni.

Breaking Mormon's own contributions into the subsections indicated by the original chapter breaks is helpful because it clarifies the book's general structure. Each of these three original chapters begins with narrative history and concludes with Mormon directly addressing his witness to his future readers. The first chapter (Mormon 1:1–3:22) recounts events from Mormon's own life, narrates a series of battles, and concludes with Mormon directly addressing his witness to latter-day Israel and his future Gentile readers. The second chapter (Mormon 4:1–5:24) narrates additional battles and concludes with Mormon directly addressing his witness to latter-day Lamanites and his future Gentile readers.

Part I: Mormon's Contributions

Mormon 1:1–7:10

CHAPTER I

Mormon 1:1–3:16   Narrates History

Mormon 3:17–22   Addresses Future Israelite
                                     and Gentile Readers

CHAPTER II

Mormon 4:1–5:7   Narrates History

Mormon 5:8–24   Addresses Future Lamanite
                                     and Gentile Readers

CHAPTER III

Mormon 6:1–22   Narrates History

Mormon 7:1–10   Addresses Future
                                     Lamanite Readers

Part II: Moroni's Contributions

Mormon 8:1–9:37

CHAPTER IV

Mormon 8:1–41   Offers Additional Narrative
                                     and Prophecies

Mormon 9:1–29   Addresses Future Deniers
                                     of Christ/Miracles

Mormon 9:30–37   Defends Any Imperfections
                                     in the Record

FIGURE 1 Structure of Mormon's record; original chapters in red.

The third chapter (Mormon 6:1–7:10) narrates the end of the Nephite world and concludes with Mormon directly addressing his witness to latter-day Lamanites.

15

Moroni's subsequent contribution to Mormon's book—the fourth original chapter—breaks into two parts. In the first half of this fourth chapter (Mormon 8), Moroni offers some additional history and prophesies about the coming forth of the Book of Mormon in a world saturated with hypocrites who have repurposed the church of God for their own gain. In the second half of that fourth chapter (Mormon 9), Moroni directly addresses his latter-day readers with targeted messages for those who do not believe in Christ and those who do not believe in the continuing reality of revelations or miracles. He concludes with a brief apologia for any imperfections in the record.

In broad strokes, then, the bones and joints that order the book's composition look like FIGURE 1 (left page).

While it is not unusual for Mormon to briefly interrupt his larger abridgement of the Nephite record to explicitly draw conclusions for his readers (e.g., Alma 28:13, "And thus we see how great the inequality of man is because of sin and transgression"), his willingness to break the narrative's fourth wall to repeatedly and substantially address an array of future readers is the defining feature of the structure of his book as a witness. As his world ends, Mormon isn't satisfied to describe what happened in the past. He is driven, rather, to use his history to intervene in the future. He positions his own book as a temporal bridge that can short circuit time and collapse the distance between himself and his future readers. Adding to Mormon's record, Moroni memorably describes this kind of direct engagement with the future when he says, "Behold, I speak unto you as if ye were present, and yet ye are not. But behold, Jesus Christ hath shown you unto me, and I know your doing" (Mormon 8:35). In this respect, Mormon engineers his book not only to chronicle history but to function as a directly addressed, present tense witness of Christ.

16

3

A Narrative Synopsis

"Lord, make me to know mine end, and the measure of
my days, what it is; that I may know how frail I am."
—Psalms 39:4

Before considering how Mormon's life and witness exemplify key elements of Christian discipleship, I want to offer a clean summary of the apocalyptic history narrated in his book. Filtering out Mormon's prophetic commentary and clarifying his timeline, I want to straightforwardly retell the story he tells. What, in Mormon's case, does the end of the world actually look like?

Initially, the end of the world looks like a ten-year-old boy. It looks like a world where a ten-year-old boy is already God's best (or last or only?) option for preserving, completing, and abridging the Nephite records. Ammaron, keeper of these records, hides them in a hill called Shim, in a land called Antum. Circa 320 AD, he gives ten-year-old Mormon a charge to carefully observe the history of his people and then, at the age of twenty-four, to retrieve the large plates of Nephi from their hiding place in the hill and record his observations. Mormon accepts this call. He explains his unlikely selection for this important job by way of Ammaron's observation that he was "a sober child" and "quick to observe" (Mormon 1:2). Ammaron's selection of a ten-year-old boy (however sober and quick to observe) may also be related to the fact that Mormon was "a descendent of Nephi" (Mormon 1:5) and, thus, plausibly enjoyed the kind of social, political, and economic advantages that would account for his literacy and, at least in part, his meteoric rise to command the Nephite armies at the age of fifteen. If so, then Mormon's being "large in stature" may be as much socio-political as physical (Mormon 2:1). Similarly, while the Lamanites are repeatedly described as having a king (cf. Mormon 2:9, 3:4, 6:2), the vacuum of political authority among the Nephites (apart from Mormon's explicitly military authority) is conspicuous. Mormon never mentions any Nephite leaders (political or military) apart from himself. Descended from a line of Nephite kings, everything appears to run through him.

At the age of eleven, Mormon is carried southward by his father to the land of Zarahemla. Zarahemla is a flashpoint and, given that war breaks out this same year, it seems likely that Mormon's father was migrating to Zarahemla in response to a call to prepare for war. The fact that at this time "the whole face of the land had become covered with buildings, and the people were as numerous almost, as it were the sand of the sea" hints that overpopulation, deforestation, and environmental degradation may have played a role in lighting the fuse (Mormon 1:7). It is unclear who started this war, but a number of battles centered on the waters of Sidon ensue. The Nephites ultimately prevail in this early conflict but Mormon's father (perhaps killed in battle) is never mentioned again. The resulting cease-fire lasts four years.

At the age of fifteen, Mormon is "visited of the Lord, and tasted and knew of the goodness of Jesus" (Mormon 1:15). Mormon, in response to this visitation, wants to preach repentance but is forbidden because the Nephites have willfully rebelled against God. Wickedness abounds, the land is infested with Gadianton robbers, treasures become slippery, and the

Three Nephites are withdrawn. This same year, "there began to be a war again" (Mormon 2:1). Described in the passive voice ("there began to be a war again"), the instigator of this second conflict is also unclear, lending the conflict an air of impersonal inevitability. Mormon is—surprisingly and without any battle-tested experience—appointed as the leader of all the Nephite armies. At the age of sixteen, he leads them into battle for the first time. The results of this first battle are not reported.

When he turns seventeen, the Lamanites return in force and Mormon's armies flee in terror. They retreat northward, occupy the city of Angolah, and fortify it. Whether the inhabitants of Angolah welcomed these armies or were forcibly displaced is unreported. The Lamanites, however, drive the Nephite army out of Angolah, then again out of the land of David. Mormon's armies regroup in the land of Joshua. They attempt to gather in their people as fast as possible but the land of Joshua is already filled with robbers and Lamanites. Chaos engulfs the region "and it was one complete revolution throughout all the face of the land" (Mormon 2:8). Mormon's initial campaigns, as far as he describes them, consist of a series of ugly defeats in which "blood and carnage spread throughout all the face of the land" (Mormon 2:8).

All of this unfolds over the span of three years until, at the age of twenty, Mormon wins his first battle with an army of 42,000 against an army of 44,000. In the glow of this victory, the Nephites appear ready to repent and Mormon is tempted to rejoice. However, Mormon's "joy was vain, for their sorrowing was not unto repentance...it was rather the sorrowing of the damned" (Mormon 2:13). In the face of this disappointment, Mormon then glosses the next fourteen years of continual horror in a single sentence: "I saw that the day of grace was passed with them, both temporally and spiritually; for I saw thousands of them hewn down in open rebellion against their God, and heaped up as dung upon the face of the land" (Mormon 2:15).

At the age of thirty-five, Mormon reports that his Nephites are now in full flight from the Lamanites and have retreated as far north as the city of Jashon, near the hill Shim, in the land of Antum where Ammaron had hidden the records. Mormon reports that he had previously gone to the hill to retrieve the large plates of Nephi and had added to that record. The Nephites continue to be hunted and driven even farther north to the land Shem. They occupy and fortify the city of Shem and gather as many people as possible.

When Mormon turns thirty-six, the Lamanites advance again. Mormon exhorts his army of 30,000 to stand against the 50,000 coming against them, urging them to "fight for their wives, and their children, and their houses, and their homes" (Mormon 2:23). However, after more than fifteen years of continual war, bloodshed, robbery, revolution, and flight, it is hard to imagine what sort of traditional homes or intact family life Mormon could be urging them to protect. The loss and chaos must have already been catastrophic. Still, Mormon's exhortation is effective and the Lamanites are repelled. Seizing their advantage, the Nephites, over the next three years, push back the Lamanites "until we had again taken possession of the lands of our inheritance" (Mormon 2:27). This victory, though, is short-lived. The following year, at the age of forty, Mormon accepts a treaty that rolls back their reclaimed lands to the narrow passage that bottle-necks the north from the south and, in the process, wholly cedes the traditionally Nephite lands of Zarahemla and Bountiful to the Lamanites and Gadiantons.

A ten year hiatus follows—"peace" seems too strong a word for this interval—in which Mormon, approaching fifty, directs his people to spend their time "preparing their lands and their arms against the time of battle" (Mormon 3:1). The operative assumption appears to be that further conflict is inevitable. The war isn't over, it has only been temporarily suspended. As a result, the Nephites do not return wholesale to normal peacetime activities but remain in a defensive crouch. During this same interval, Mormon is also finally commanded to once again cry repentance to his people. His efforts, however, are vain and the people, collectively waiting for the hammer of war to fall once more, harden their hearts.

At the age of fifty, Mormon receives an epistle from the king of the Lamanites declaring that hostilities are about to resume. In response, Mormon gathers his people to the land Desolation in order to position them at the north/south bottleneck. They fortify with all their might.

As Mormon turns fifty-one, the Lamanites attack but are repelled. As he turns fifty-two, the Lamanites attack again and are repelled again. Goaded by these victories, the Nephites begin to boast in their own strength and "swear before the heavens that they would avenge themselves of the blood of their brethren who had been slain by their enemies" (Mormon 3:9). Mormon, appalled, "did utterly refuse from this time forth to be a commander and a leader of this people" (Mormon 3:11). He will have nothing to do with the project of revenge.

In the years that follow, Mormon stands as an idle witness. At the age of fifty-three he watches as the Nephites leave the relative safety of their fortifications in Desolation and go out against the Lamanites. Unsurprisingly, the Nephites are driven back. A second

Lamanite army overtakes them and many are slain or taken captive. Those who survive flee to the city of Teancum.

At the age of fifty-four, Mormon watches as the Lamanites attack Teancum. The Nephites drive the Lamanites back and, pursuing them, also retake the city Desolation. Thousands are slain on both sides. Two years after that initial assault on Teancum, the Lamanites attack again. This time, Mormon reports, "it is impossible for the tongue to describe, or for man to write a perfect description of the horrible scene of the blood and carnage which was among the people, both of the Nephites and of the Lamanites; and every heart was hardened, so that they delighted in the shedding of blood continually" (Mormon 4:11). In short, Mormon says, "there never had been so great wickedness among all the children of Lehi, nor even among all the house of Israel" (Mormon 4:12). With a massive numerical advantage, the Lamanites retake the city Desolation and then finally capture the city Teancum. In the process, they took "many prisoners both women and children, and did offer them up as sacrifices unto their idol gods" (Mormon 4:14). Furious, the Nephites counter-attack and reacquire Teancum and Desolation in the following year.

Over the next eight years, until Mormon turns sixty-five, the status quo holds. The deadlock is broken, however, when the Lamanites come down again, now with an uncountable host, and the Nephites "began to be swept off by them even as a dew before the sun" (Mormon 4:18). The Lamanites take Desolation. The Nephites retreat to Boaz and hold firm. The Lamanites come a second time against Boaz and the city falls. "The Nephites were driven and slaughtered with an exceedingly great slaughter; their women and their children were again sacrificed unto idols" (Mormon 4:21). Everyone flees. Mormon, fearing that the Lamanites are about to overtake the hill Shim where the records are hidden, secures them.

At the age of sixty-five—with the records secure, with the Lamanites pressing deeper into the north, and with the Nephites in dire straits—Mormon repents of his oath to no longer lead the armies of his people and resumes command. Knowing, though, that his people will not repent and that divine judgment is unavoidable, he does so "without hope" for any lasting success (Mormon 5:2). When the Lamanites attack the city of Jordan, the Nephites hold their ground and, thus, shield the remaining lands to the north. However, all the abandoned lands to the south "were destroyed by the Lamanites, and their towns, and villages, and cities were burned with fire," reducing them to scorched earth and ashes (Mormon 5:5). All of this occupies Mormon's life from the age of sixty-five to the age of seventy.

At the age of seventy, Mormon's tenuous control of his defensive line is challenged. The Lamanites attack Jordan and overwhelm the Nephites with vastly superior numbers. They tread the Nephites beneath their feet. The Nephites are again in full flight. Every man, woman, or child too slow to flee the breaking wave of destruction is "swept down and destroyed" (Mormon 5:7).

On the run, a seventy-year-old Mormon writes a letter petitioning the Lamanite king to give the Nephites a chance to regroup and gather all their remaining armies to the hill Cumorah in the land of Cumorah. The Lamanite king agrees. Mormon hopes to use the hill and the surrounding waters to his tactical advantage. Mormon gathers his people for four consecutive years. This gathering appears to be definitive. All Nephites are gathered in. At the age of seventy-four, knowing that he "began to be old; and knowing it to be the last struggle of my people," Mormon largely completes the additional abridgement of Nephite records that we know as the Book of Mormon (Mormon 6:6). He arranges to entrust this abridgment to Moroni and hides the remainder of the records in Cumorah.

Having gathered his people and completed his final preparations, Mormon reports that "it came to pass that my people, with their wives and their children, did now behold the armies of the Lamanites marching towards them; and with that awful fear of death which fills the breasts of all the wicked, did they await to receive them" (Mormon 6:7). The battle commences and the Nephites are summarily hewn down. Mormon is wounded, falls among the corpses, and is momentarily spared because he is mistaken for dead. Save twenty-four people, all of Mormon's forces—approaching a quarter million dead, not counting Nephite women and children—"had fallen; and their flesh, and bones, and blood lay upon the face of the earth, being left by the hands of those who slew them to molder upon the land, and to crumble and to return to their mother earth" (Mormon 6:15).

As he surveys this apocalyptic scene, Mormon's soul is "rent with anguish, because of the slain of my people" (Mormon 6:16). This anguish wrings from him one final lament:

> O ye fair ones, how could ye have departed from the ways of the Lord! O ye fair ones, how could ye have rejected that Jesus, who stood with open arms to receive you! Behold, if ye had not done this, ye would not have fallen. But behold, ye are fallen, and I mourn your loss. O ye fair sons and daughters, ye fathers and mothers, ye husbands and wives, ye fair

ones, how is that ye could have fallen! But behold, ye are gone, and my sorrows cannot bring your return (Mormon 6:17–20).

In the aftermath of this final battle, Moroni records that those who escaped were hunted "until they were all destroyed" (Mormon 8:2). Mormon was among them. "My father also was killed by them," Moroni writes, "and I even remain alone to write the sad tale of the destruction of my people" (Mormon 8:3).

4

Witness

"Something always remains. The witness is this remnant."
—Giorgio Agamben

Mormon's world comes to a quick and brutal end. With surprising speed, his civilization collapses. He lives through the loss of all things. With his life back-lit by this apocalyptic light, what aspects of Christian discipleship are thrown into sharp relief? If Christian discipleship sits squarely at the crossroads of a world that imposes the loss of all things and a religion that requires the sacrifice of all things, what does it look like to willingly lose all things? What does it look like to practice that loss as discipleship? What does it look like for Mormon to intentionally take up his cross and follow Jesus?

Mormon's discipleship depends, first and foremost, on his willingness to witness the end of the world. His willingness to sacrifice all things is rooted in his willingness to unflinchingly witness the passing away of all things. He transfigures sheer loss into consecrated sacrifice through faithful witness. This, as we will see, is what most fundamentally distinguishes the narrow path of the disciple from the way of the world. The disciple, rather than fleeing or denying the end of the world, bears witness to this deep truth about life: that everything with a beginning has an end.

As a result, the first step to caring for and consecrating this world's passing is to resolutely witness that passing. Sidestepping the lure of freeze-framed fantasies and candy-colored distractions, the most basic act of discipleship is to forget ourselves and pay careful attention. As Mormon describes it, his job is "to manifest unto the world the things which I saw and heard" and to give this witness "according to the manifestations of the Spirit" (Mormon 3:16). If Mormon is able to console the broken hearted and to mourn with those that mourn, it is because he has been willingly sensitized to how—day after day, hour after hour, moment after moment—the world is ceaselessly created, dissolved, and recreated.

How is Mormon able to do this? What fits him for this work of witnessing? In light of Mormon's commission to witness, Ammaron's initial description of the ten year-old boy acquires additional significance. "I perceive," Ammaron says, "that thou art a sober child, and art quick to observe" (Mormon 1:2). Mormon is fitted for the work of witnessing by the fact that he is "sober" and by the fact that he is "quick to observe." His lived experience of discipleship hinges on pairing a certain mood (his sobriety) with a certain intensity of perception (his quickness to observe) that, together, work to consecrate the loss of all things. In short, Mormon's discipleship powerfully pairs what we might describe as a divine melancholy with a deep sensitivity to the world's fragility.

In this respect, the path of Christian discipleship may broadly depend on the consistent cultivation— through prayer and fasting and study and service—of a certain mood.

It may seem unusual to claim that Mormon's mood is theologically crucial to his discipleship but, in my view, it is impossible to adequately understand the forces at play in redemption without accounting for moods and emotions. To clarify why, briefly consider, in general, the importance of moods to human experience.

I take it for granted that moods, emotions, and affects are not just existential window dressing. They don't just add a little subjective "color" to what would otherwise be an accurate, dispassionate, objective experience of the world. Rather, I take it for granted that moods and emotions are crucial neurological mechanisms for focusing human perceptions and driving human actions. As a result, I understand moods and emotions to be fundamental to any human experience of truth and meaning. Human experiences of any kind—including those we describe as objective—are all impossible without moods and emotions.[1]

Moods and emotions are modes of perception. They make truth possible. They disclose the world. They are fundamental forms of attunement and orientation that operate a notch lower than conscious thoughts and decisions. Like the dial on an analog radio, moods tune the mind to certain stations of perception. They select relevant slices of sensation and information from the pressing static and chaos of the wider world.

Moods and emotions are a body's initial, gut-level read on what, in that moment, is *relevant*. They function as filters and, thus, make meaning possible. Meaning depends on having some criteria for screening what information is currently relevant and what is not. Moods and emotions sort and prioritize information, they bring a particular profile of experience into meaningful focus and they motivate us to act on that information.

It's clear that someone who feels angry, someone who feels fear, and someone who feels compassion will experience the same situation in profoundly different ways. The elements of the situation that stand out as relevant will vary widely and, in turn, the sorts of motivated actions that seem appropriate will vary widely. Though the situation may be otherwise identical, anger will filter perceptions and shape actions in one way, fear will filter perceptions and shape actions in a second way, and compassion will filter perceptions and shape actions in a third.

Given how crucial moods, emotions, and feelings are to experiences of any kind, it should come as no surprise that they are also crucial to religious experience. Moreover, if discipleship turns on reshaping and reordering human experience at the deepest levels, then moods and emotions ought to be *doubly* crucial to religious experiences. It should also come as no surprise, then, that recognizing the baseline persistence of a certain mood in Mormon's own life is crucial to recognizing how his life brings key elements of Christian discipleship into sharp focus.

Understood in these terms, discipleship doesn't just depend on a certain way of acting. It depends on a certain mood or bearing. It depends on a certain way of holding time as it passes, on a certain tendency of thought to circle back to the same bare and quiet space, on a certain unclenching of the mental fist. It depends on a continual tilting of the soul, regardless of what thoughts and feelings play across the surface of the mind, toward a certain primal mood. Sobriety is a good name for this baseline Christian mood, for the disciple's default inclination of heart and orientation of mind. Divine melancholy is another. Mormon embodies this melancholic sobriety and his attunement to the Spirit—to life and light and suffering and loss—is, as a practical matter, grounded in this bearing.

This divine melancholy isn't the same thing as clinical depression, anxiety, or post-traumatic stress. These real and painfully common sorts of suffering need medical attention as surely as cancer or a broken arm. Divine melancholy, on the other hand, as a habitual bearing, doesn't exclude the possibility of peace and joy. In fact, unafraid of the truth about this world's passing, this sobriety is ultimately the only thing that makes real joy possible. It gives substance to what would otherwise be fleeting and it prompts us to appreciate what would otherwise be unsatisfying. As the world filters through us, this melancholy disposes us to handle its passing with tender and grateful care. It gives us eyes to see what, in our vanity, we would otherwise fail to see. This sensitized mood amplifies our ability to perceive and these amplified perceptions, in turn, feed back into an increasingly sensitized mood. A feedback loop structures the relationship between Mormon's sobriety and his swiftness to observe. He is quick to observe because he is sober and he is sober because he is so quick to observe.

It makes sense, then, that Mormon would explicitly invoke his sobriety a second time in Mormon 1:15 as the only plausible explanation for why he was personally visited by Jesus: "And I, being fifteen years of age and being somewhat of a sober mind, *therefore* I was visited of the Lord, and tasted and knew of the goodness of Jesus" (emphasis added). In this case, Mormon's "sober mind" allowed him to see what others failed to notice: that they, like him, "might have been clasped in the arms of Jesus" (Mormon 5:11). His divine melancholy sensitized him to God's urgent and available goodness. Mormon, like his master, was "a man of sorrows, and acquainted with grief," and so, while the rest of us "hid as it were our faces from him," Mormon was instead able to see the face of God (Isaiah 53:3).

When we hide our faces from sorrow and suffering and pretend that the world is not ending, we hide our faces from God. Then, numb and displeased and distracted—graceless and oblivious and entitled—we fail to taste life's goodness. We fail to bear witness to what's given and to what, in its givenness, is passing away.

"The work of miracles and of healing did cease" among the Nephites, Mormon observes, because as far as his people were capable of seeing, "there *were* no gifts from the Lord" (Mormon 1:13, 14, emphasis added). Lacking an attuned sobriety, the Nephites were blind to the gifts and healing that God offered. They were incapable of witnessing his miracles.

There is a deep connection between Mormon's mood and his mindfulness. His sobriety is paired with his calling to witness. His melancholy bearing is paired with his intensity of perception. These two elements are so tightly intertwined that, for Mormon, the work of Christian discipleship necessarily unfolds as the work of witnessing. In this way, Mormon models discipleship. To be a disciple of Christ is to live, like Mormon, as a witness. And living as a witness hinges on two things: the cultivation of a certain mood and the cultivation of a certain intensity of perception. It hinges on being sober and on being quick to observe. It hinges on a willingness to witness (rather than hide our faces from) the end of the world.

5

Creation

"This world...was ever, is now, and ever shall be an ever-living fire, with measures of it kindling, and measures going out." —*Heraclitus*

Why, on scales both large and small, is the world perpetually passing away? Why, like Mormon, must we lose all things?

The world is perpetually passing away because it is, simultaneously, perpetually beginning. The end of the world is ongoing because God's work of creating the world is ongoing. God not only created the world (in the past tense), he is *continually* creating the world (in the present tense). New lives and forms of life surge forth and old lives and forms of life pass away, each dependent on the other. The world is planted, it sprouts, it seeds, and fades. The world is born, it grows, it couples, and yields. Everything is in motion. Everything differs from itself. Life and death are intertwined. "I tell you the solemn truth," Jesus warns, "unless a kernel of wheat falls into the ground and dies, it remains by itself alone. But if it dies, it produces much grain" (John 12:24, NET).

If, as Joseph Smith taught, God didn't spontaneously create the world out of nothing—if, in the beginning, God found himself *already* in the midst of matter and intelligence—then every act of creation must be understood as an act of recreation. The work of organizing matter is, necessarily, the work of reorganizing matter.

And if all creation is recreation, then God's creative work may not only be unfinished, it may be unfinishable. Given that there is no end to God's work and glory, his creative work may never conclude. In this case, the world will only continue to grow from one grace and glory to the next—with the flipside being that, for as long as God continues to re/create the world, the world will also continue to end. Every new act of creation will, at minimum, impose itself as the partial loss of what came before. Every new world will unfold, inescapably, as the passing away of the old. We will always find ourselves, at least in part, in the same position as Mormon: witnesses to the end of the world.

Although God's work of re/creation is glorious and redemptive, it is also hard. Although it is joyful, it is also sobering. As a result, the path of discipleship is hard. The work of witnessing God's creative work is hard. The call to participate in this work of creation is hard. Taking up this cross is hard. And—certainly—*being* created (and recreated) is hard.

Christian discipleship is the work of willingly participating in the re/creation of the world. It's the work of willingly participating in the world's passing away. And this willing participation is what consecrates the world's passing and renders it sacred. A disciple's job is to continually inherit the new worlds that God is creating (now, today) by continually sacrificing (again) our claims to the old.

When we refuse to sacrifice all things, when we refuse to willingly witness the end of the world, we refuse to willingly participate in the world's re/creation. And when we refuse to participate in the world's re/creation, we refuse to acknowledge its Creator. As Moroni argues at length in Mormon 9:7–20, this refusal to acknowledge the Creator tends to take a specific form: it tends to condense into a concentrated refusal

37

to acknowledge that God, as the re/Creator, *continues* to be a God of miracles. Refusing the ongoing miracle of re/creation, we imagine "up unto [ourselves] a god who is not a God of miracles" (Mormon 9:10). Or, to the same effect, we might imagine up unto ourselves a safer God who was a God of miracles (but no longer is), a safer God who once spoke (but no longer speaks), or a safer God who created in the past (but no longer creates and recreates).

But, in the end, these denials all amount to the same thing. When we deny that God's creative work is ongoing, we also deny his present availability. We deny his most obvious and insistent manifestation in the world. As Paul says: "For the invisible things of him from the creation of the world are clearly seen, being understood by the things that are made, even his eternal power and Godhead" (Romans 1:20). Or as Alma puts it: "All things denote there is a God; yea, even the earth, and all things that are upon the face of it, yea, and its motion, yea, and also all the planets which move in their regular form do witness that there is a Supreme Creator....Will ye deny against all these witnesses?" (Alma 30:44–45). When, as sinners, we deny these witnesses—when we fail to join them as witnesses—we've "changed the truth of God into a lie, and worshipped and served the creature more than the Creator" (Romans 1:25).

When, in response to these denials of God's continuing work in the world, Moroni offers to "show unto [us] a God of miracles," he doesn't resort to recounting the rare sorts of supernatural interventions we might expect (Mormon 9:11). Surprisingly, in Mormon 9 he doesn't offer anything like the extended recitation of wonders that he gives in Ether 12:6–22 when he recounts a litany of miraculous healings, conversions, escapes, and visions wrought by faith. Instead, avoiding what we normally think of as miracles, he focuses on two specific examples of God's miraculous work: creation and resurrection. "I will show unto you a God of miracles," Moroni says, "and it is that same God who created the heavens and the earth, and all things that in them are" (Mormon 9:11). To drive this point home, Moroni directly addresses our expected skepticism that the created world—ordinary and mundane and obvious as it is—counts as a miracle:

> Behold, are not the things that God hath wrought marvelous in our eyes? Yea, and who can comprehend the marvelous works of God? Who shall say that it was not a miracle that by his word the heaven and the earth should be; and by the power of his word man was created of the dust of the earth; and by the power of his word have miracles been wrought? (Mormon 9:16–17)

On Moroni's account, if God's ongoing work of re/creation doesn't appear to us to be miraculous, the problem is ours, not God's. "Are not the things that God hath wrought marvelous in our eyes" (Mormon 9:16)? If we deny that God's works are marvelous, the problem is with our eyes. The problem stems from our failure to witness. We've failed to be sober and we've failed to observe. "The reason why he ceaseth to do miracles among the children of men is because that they dwindle in unbelief, and depart from the right way, and know not the God in whom they should trust" (Mormon 9:20).

We fail to see the miracles right in front of our eyes because we dwindle in unbelief. We know not the God in whom we should trust. Desensitized to the divine, we are willfully blind. We intentionally turn away. We deliberately close our eyes. In this respect, Moroni offers a solid definition of what it means to dwindle in unbelief: to dwindle in unbelief is to fail to see God's ongoing and ordinary work of re/creation as a miracle.

Again, however, it's no surprise that we would shy away from the work of faithfully witnessing the world's continual creation, dissolution, and recreation. And given how hard it is to witness the end of the world, it's no surprise that we are reluctant to believe that there isn't some other way, that there isn't some shortcut to salvation that might bypass the need to sacrifice all things. Searching for this kind of shortcut, we might imagine up unto ourselves a god who is not a God of miracles, a god who doesn't ceaselessly re/create the world. We might imagine up unto ourselves a god who, at the very least, exempted *himself* from the hard work of witnessing and sacrificing.

But this is not the case. God—Immanuel—is in the world with us. Consider Moroni's second example of a miracle. In addition to the miracle of creation, Moroni's other example of God's miraculous work is Christ's own death and resurrection.

> But behold, I will show unto you a God of miracles, even the God of Abraham, and the God of Isaac, and the God of Jacob; and it is that same God who created the heavens and the earth, and all things that in them are. Behold, he created Adam, and by Adam came the fall of man. And because of the fall of man came Jesus Christ, even the Father and the Son; and because of Jesus Christ came the redemption of man. And because of the redemption of man, which came by Jesus Christ, they are brought back into the presence of the Lord; yea, this is wherein all men are redeemed,

because the death of Christ bringeth to pass the resurrection, which bringeth to pass a redemption from an endless sleep. (Mormon 9:11–13)

Moroni draws a straight line from God's work of creation, through Adam's fall, to the necessity of the world's re/creation in Christ. He draws a straight line from the creation of the world, through the fall of man, to Christ's own willingness to sacrifice all things. In this way, Christ's sacrifice and resurrection not only promise to redeem us and recreate us, they affirm that God is himself a willing participant in both the work of creation and the necessity of recreation. God himself witnesses, sacrifices, dies, and is resurrected. There is no plan B. There is no other world—frozen and sheltered and uncreated—where creation and growth and progression and recreation are not the order of the day. There are no worlds (or even Gods) exempt from loss and sacrifice. The heavens, sober and observant, also weep (cf. Moses 7:28–40).

By framing re/creation itself as the miracle *par excellence*, Moroni also clarifies what it means for God to witness his own creative work and, despite the costs, still pronounce that work good: "And God saw every thing that he had made, and, behold, it was very good" (Genesis 1:31).

Strikingly, Moroni couples his insistence that creation is itself the fundamental expression of God's miraculous power with his insistence that God *continues* to be a God of miracles. "And if there were miracles wrought then," he asks, "why has God ceased to be a God of miracles and yet be an unchangeable Being? And behold, I say unto you he changeth not; if so he would cease to be God; and he ceaseth not to be God, and is a God of miracles" (Mormon 9:19). God, as the

God of miracles, doesn't cease to do miracles. And God, as the Creator, doesn't cease to create. If he ceased to miraculously create, he would cease to be God.

But if God doesn't cease to create, then what does it mean for God to witness "every thing that he had made, and, behold, it was very good" (Genesis 1:31)? If, despite all its goodness, the created world is itself perpetually dissolved and re/created, then what does it mean for that world to be very good? If it was good, why must it pass away? And if it was already good, why does God continue to re/create?

We might pose the question this way: when God witnesses the work of creation and calls it very good, what *exactly* is being named as good?

By framing creation itself as a miracle, Moroni is urging us to see the created world with new eyes. He is urging us to stop taking the world for granted, to stop looking past it or through it as something boring or obvious, and to witness it, instead, as the continually fresh miracle that it is. He's urging us to see, in each created thing, the always lingering halo of its ongoing and miraculous re/creation. Rather than seeing miracles as *exceptions* to the rule of creation, Moroni is arguing that the *fact* of creation is itself miraculous. If we can learn to see the created world as a miracle, then the created world will itself shine with the aura of the miraculous work that creates it. We will learn to witness not just the product but the process. We will learn to witness not just the outcome but the action. And, to the degree that the ongoing work of creation shines through each created but unfinished thing, the Creator will himself come into view. "The invisible things of him" will now be clearly seen in the visibility of the "things that are made" (Romans 1:20).

When this happens, rather than clinging to the goodness of any one of these visibly created things, we will learn to trust God as the Creator and affirm the more fundamental goodness of the *work* of creation itself, open-ended as it is. We will be willing to witness the end of the world and sacrifice all things because we will recognize that God's goodness is more deeply and substantially expressed in the ongoing *process* of creation than in any temporary, local expressions of that creativity. Witnessed as a miracle, creation will show up as a living, present tense verb rather than as an orphaned assortment of nouns that could be collected and squirreled away. We will learn to echo God's witness that his creations are "very good" by affirming that this goodness is always rooted in the work of creating, dissolving, and recreating the world.

To return then to my previous question: in order to join God in witnessing that his creation is very good, *what* must be affirmed as good? What exactly needs to be affirmed? It seems clear that we must bear witness not only to the goodness of what is created but—more profoundly and fundamentally and wholeheartedly—to the difficult, costly, and glorious creative process itself. Witnessing that the creative process is itself the source of the created world's goodness, we will be empowered to witness the end of the world with grace and charity. We'll be empowered to willingly sacrifice all things as part of the divine effort to re/create all things.

6

Treasures

"Grant me the treasure of sublime poverty."
—Francis of Assisi

What happens when we put our trust in the fragility of created things rather than in God's ongoing work of creation and recreation? What does it look like when, rather than practicing sacrifice, we deny that the world is passing away, deny that we will lose everything, and deny that the creation of the world is ongoing?

The answer is sin. Sin is, at bottom, the business of living in denial. It's a failure to witness. As a bone-deep existential bearing, sin is a complex but self-reinforcing feedback loop of ideas, intentions, emotions, actions, moods, and inherited strategies geared to accomplish one thing: to refuse, with a fisted grip, the end of the world. Sin refuses re/creation. Sin, as the Christian tradition at large has long insisted, is what happens when we choose to love the fragility of created things more than the Creator and his enduring work of re/creation. Sin is what happens when, as we've already seen Paul claim, we have "changed the truth of God into a lie, and worshipped and served the creature more than the Creator" (Romans 1:25).

To live this way—to live in denial of the world's continual creation, dissolution, and recreation—is to live as the damned.

Those who are damned aim to acquire as many created things as possible, to wring as much satisfaction from them as possible, and to keep these things and satisfactions for as long as possible. They aim to generate and perpetuate an illusion of ownership, permanence, and control. Rather than mirroring God's own joyful but sober work of witnessing, sacrificing, and recreating, sinners fancifully project themselves into the imaginary (and idolatrous) position they wish God occupied: the pseudo-divine position of a safely enthroned proprietor who exercises complete control over a frozen reality. Flinching from the necessity of re/creation and denying the necessity of sacrifice, the damned ironically consign themselves to the dissolution of the world they reflexively wanted to preserve. They consign themselves to the horror of living through the world's dissolution *without* willingly participating in the redemption and re/creation of that continually dissolving world. Rather than cultivating a sobriety capable of "sorrowing ... unto repentance," they are instead condemned to experience "the sorrowing of the damned" (Mormon 2:13).

This is to say that, rather than experiencing God's work of creating and recreating the world as inherently good, the damned experience this world-in-progress as cursed. This, Mormon reports, is exactly what happens to his own people. They experience the world's continual passing as a curse rather than a grace. As a result, their world ends catastrophically rather than redemptively because they are too deeply invested in projecting and maintaining a contrived illusion of comfort, permanence, and control. They "built up" lives unto themselves "to get gain" and, as a result, they caused "great pollutions upon the face of the earth" (cf. Mormon 8:33, 31). Refusing to sacrifice, they aimed to acquire and consume.

This project of acquisition, though, is doomed to fail. And it is doomed to fail by the very forces of re/

creation that motivate the desire to get gain and stock-
pile treasures in the first place. In Mormon 1:17–2:14,
Mormon offers a case study in this doomed project of
acquiring treasure. Witnessing the decline of his people, he sees how the Nephites hardened their hearts
against the work of their Creator and how "because of
the hardness of their hearts the land was cursed for
their sake" (Mormon 1:17).

Mormon's description of how the land was cursed
"for their sake" could be read in several ways. First, it
is possible to read this explanation as simply a com-
ment on why God chose to curse the land: it's cursed
in order to punish the hard-hearted. But in light of
what I've already argued, we might also offer a second
reading: that God intends this curse to be a kind of
blessing, that he cursed the land for their benefit. He
cursed the land in an effort to pry from their fists the
damning fantasy that, under normal circumstances, it
would be possible to avoid the work of sacrifice and
succeed, instead, at the project of acquisition.

Or, perhaps even more straightforwardly, we might
offer a third, complimentary reading that simply takes
this experience of a curse as what naturally happens
when the world is seen through the lens of a hard
heart. Read along these lines, God wouldn't be seen to
intervene here in any unusual way to additionally curse
the land. Rather, the mistake of seeing God's work of
re/creation as a curse would simply be the inevitable
result of a hard heart that persistently refused to willingly witness the world's passing. Unless we are willing
to sacrifice all things, the loss of all things will inevitably show itself as a terrible curse.

For the Nephites, the loss of all things is personified by the Gadianton robbers. "These Gadianton robbers, who were among the Lamanites, did infest the
land" (Mormon 1:18). For the damned, the whole world

seems to be full of thieves and robbers, forever stealing everything they love. Like a plague, these robbers infest every nook and cranny of creation. Everywhere they turn, the Nephites find themselves robbed of the treasures and satisfactions they had hoped to keep. Everywhere they look, the world is passing away. Everywhere they turn, the world is continually slipping through their fingers. The omnipresence of these robbers prompts the Nephites "to hide up their treasures in the earth," but the earth itself proves no more accommodating than the robbers (Mormon 1:18). Once buried, these treasures "became slippery, because the Lord had cursed the land, that they could not hold them, nor retain them again" (Mormon 1:18).

Mormon then reports that the slipperiness of these treasures is additionally connected with the fact that "there were sorceries, and witchcrafts, and magics; and the power of the evil one was wrought upon all the face of the land, even unto the fulfilling of all the words of Abinadi, and also Samuel the Lamanite" (Mormon 1:19). What role do sorceries and witchcrafts and magics play in the loss of these treasures? The most obvious reading is that magic made these treasures slippery. It was because of magic and sorcery that, once buried, these treasures could not be kept or recovered because the robbers were themselves using witchcraft to cause the treasures to disappear into the earth.

But given the ambiguity of the verse, we might also read magic and sorcery as a Nephite *response* to the problem of the robbers. We might read magic as a security protocol. In this case, in an effort to prevent the world from passing away, the Nephites resort to magic. They deploy a kind of dark pseudo-priesthood that taps into "the power of the evil one" in a futile effort to shore up their denial of the world's passing and preserve the illusion of ownership and mastery. If true priesthood practices sacrifice, magic practices anti-sacrifice. Rather than sacrificing, it sequesters. Rather than giving, it withholds. If magic and sorcery enter the Nephite picture as a form of anti-sacrifice, then that plan predictably backfires. Using magical thinking to prop up the fantasy that sacrifice is optional can only make things worse. Magical thinking can only hasten the loss of all things by souring re/creation into sheer ruin. As Mormon makes clear, despite all this magic and sorcery, the Nephite treasures are still lost. They still slip away. And to make matters worse, these same Nephite denials have now compounded their losses by simultaneously unleashing the nihilating power of the evil one upon the land.

On either reading of magic, Mormon reports that this wholesale loss of treasure means that "all the words of Abinadi, and also Samuel the Lamanite," are fulfilled (Mormon 1:19). The specific Abinadite prophecy Mormon has in mind is unclear, but Samuel's own predictions are easy to identify. In Helaman 13, Samuel clearly predicts the end of Nephite world. "Four hundred years shall not pass away," God warns the Nephites through Samuel, "before I will cause that they shall be smitten" (Helaman 13:9). More to the point, as this world ends,

> a curse shall come upon the land .... the day shall come that they shall hide up their treasures, because they have set their hearts upon riches; and because they have set their hearts upon their riches, and will hide up their treasures when they shall flee before their enemies; because they will not hide them up unto me, cursed be they and also their treasures; and in that day shall they be smitten, saith the Lord. (Helaman 13:17, 20)

Here, the curse of slippery treasures is tightly tied to the fact that the hearts of the people were set upon these treasures. To the degree that the people "hide up" treasures unto *themselves*, the treasures are forfeit. For "he that hideth not up his treasures unto me, cursed is he, and also the treasure" (Helaman 13:19). But to the degree that "they shall hide up their treasures unto me," the Lord promises, those treasures can be redeemed (Helaman 13:19). What would it look like to hide up treasure unto yourself? It would look like denying the end of the world. Alternately, what would it look like to hide up treasure unto the Lord? It would look like abandoning the fantasy that these treasures were yours to keep in the first place. It would look like sacrificing your claim to all things. It would look like witnessing the end of the world. It would look like discipleship.

In response to how slippery their treasures have become, Mormon is briefly hopeful that this loss of all things will prompt the Nephites to return to the redemptive work of sacrificing all things. "When I, Mormon, saw their lamentation and their mourning and their sorrow before the Lord, my heart did begin to rejoice within me, knowing the mercies and the long-suffering of the Lord" (Mormon 2:12). But his hopes are unfulfilled. This mourning doesn't grow into sobriety. Lacking faith in Christ and his sacrifice, the Nephites are unable to transfigure their own loss into sacrifice. "But behold this my joy was vain, for their sorrowing was not unto repentance, because of the goodness of God; but it was rather the sorrowing of the damned, because the Lord would not always suffer them to take happiness in sin" (Mormon 2:13).

Both the disciples and the damned experience sorrow. But the former, already grounded in a sober and melancholic bearing attuned to dissolution, are able to witness the world's passing and continue to trust in the work of re/creation. When Christ's disciples sorrow, they sorrow "unto repentance" and their sorrow is recast as a constructive form of sacrifice. For the latter, however, for those who sorrow as the damned, the world's inevitable passing is nothing but a curse and a loss. Rather than coming "unto Jesus with broken hearts and contrite spirits," the damned "curse God, and wish to die" (Mormon 2:14). Unable to see the world's passing and re/creation as anything but a curse, they can only return that same profanity, cursing God and wishing to die. Moreover, Mormon points out, despite wishing to die, "nevertheless they would struggle with the sword for their lives" (Mormon 2:14).

In Mormon 2:14, then, the Nephites exhibit two key characteristics of the damned. First, as sinners, the damned ironically go about fighting for their lives (and denying death) in a way that can only ramify death and loss. They blindly react to their loss in a way that makes the problem worse. And second, the damned's denial of the world's end—and, thus, of the Creator's ongoing work of re/creation—dependably crystallizes into the work of *cursing* the world. That is to say, their denial of death dependably curdles into a desire for revenge.

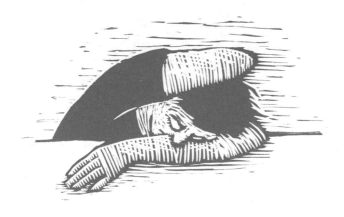

7

Without Hope

"Be intent on action, not on the fruits of action."
—*The Bhagavad Gita*

The damned, cursing their Creator and his ongoing work of re/creation, attempt to live "without Christ and God in the world" (Mormon 5:16). Their goal is to live in denial, to disavow the world's passing, and to shore up their magical thinking with an illusion-fortifying mass of treasures and satisfactions. Mormon, in contrast, treads the path of the disciple. Willing to soberly witness the end of the world, Mormon learns how to perform his actions as gestures of sacrifice. He learns how to act without expectation of gain. Counterintuitively, he learns how to act "without faith" and "without hope" and, thus, how to selflessly recenter his heart and mind on the actions themselves rather than their outcomes (cf. Mormon 3:12, 5:2). He learns how to perform acts of love and service for their own sake.

As a practical matter, the difference between the damned and the disciple hinges on the difference between these contrasting modes of subtraction: whereas the damned attempt to live *without* God, the disciple learns how to live *without* hope of gain.

Consider, first, the attempt to live without God and, thereby, avoid the loss of all things. Mormon, witnessing the "unbelief and idolatry" that saturated his world, describes how "the Spirit of the Lord hath already ceased to strive with their fathers; and they are without Christ and God in the world; and they are driven about as chaff before the wind" (Mormon 5:15, 16). Here, Mormon sandwiches his description of how the damned live without God between two additional claims. As he frames it, living without God in the world is tied to: ① the Spirit of the Lord no longer striving with you, and ② being driven about as chaff before the wind.

To live without God in the world is to live without the Spirit. It is to live without the constant re/creative push of that Spirit "striving" with you. Spirit strives. It pushes and pulls and strains. Spirit materializes at the bleeding edge of the world's re/creation. It materializes at the white-hot tip of time's spear, at the point where the future passes through the crucible of the present to become the past. And, what's more, this Spirit doesn't simply strive in the abstract. It strives, Mormon says, "with" us. It gathers. It invites and calls. It coordinates and cooperates and collaborates. Striving *with* the Spirit, we no longer live *without* Christ and God in the world. Striving with the Spirit of the Creator, we actively participate in the world's re/creation.

Living without God in the world, the damned are left to themselves. No longer striving with the Spirit, they are left alone to be "driven about as chaff before the wind" (Mormon 5:16). The losses they suffer aren't consecrated as part of the world's re/creation. Their losses are absolute. Their actions are vain. Because their actions aren't performed as sacrifice, the damned think to themselves: "do this, or do that, and it mattereth not" (Mormon 8:31). They wager their lives on the fantasies of security that success and wealth pretend to supply, only to discover that the winds of fortune blow erratically and unpredictably. In the process, they discover, as the author of Ecclesiastes puts it, that "the race is not to the swift, nor the battle to the strong, neither yet bread to the wise, nor yet riches to men of understanding, nor yet favour to men of skill; but time and chance happeneth to them all" (Ecclesiastes

9:11). Success and wealth are not inherently meaningful. Though goodness may tend toward prosperity, material prosperity isn't necessarily a bellwether of divine favor. All treasures are slippery and they cannot insulate us from the loss of all things. And deployed as an idolatrous defense against such loss, success and wealth are less than useless. They can only hasten our ruin.

As a result, Mormon continues, the damned "are led about by Satan, even as chaff is driven before the wind, or as a vessel is tossed about upon the waves, without sail or anchor, or without anything wherewith to steer her; and even as she is, so are they" (Mormon 5:18). The damned, living as if the world were not ending, are incapable of steering their lives into redemption and re/creation. They lack "anything wherewith to steer" because—given the world's continual dissolution and re/creation—life *can't* be steered clear of loss. Rather, the only possible way to steer is to steer the loss itself into a sacrificial gesture of love. The only way to strive with God is to willingly (and preemptively and redemptively and counterintuitively) steer *into* that loss by way of consecration and sacrifice. This is the path of discipleship. Walking this path, we put down the impossible burden of living in denial and, instead, find ourselves mercifully yoked with Christ and God in the redemptive work of sacrificing all things.

Consider, then, what it looks like to live, as Mormon does, through the end of the world. Consider what it looks like to live "without faith" and "without hope." In Mormon 3:12 and 5:2, Mormon uses both of these surprising and disquieting formulas to describe his work as a disciple. On my reading, these troubling formulas—working "without faith" and "without hope"—are crucial to more clearly defining how loss is transfigured into sacrifice. I would argue that Mormon's difficult and counterintuitive *subtraction* of faith and hope is what defines every sacrificial gesture. As he formulates it here (and, again, I recognize that these are unusual formulas that shouldn't be taken to undercut our obvious need for faith and hope in Christ), sheer loss becomes gracious sacrifice only when we learn how to give without hope of recovery.

Mormon uses these subtractive formulas to describe what it's like to continue loving and sacrificing even as the world ends. He uses them to describe what it looks like when, practicing an apocalyptic brand of discipleship, the apocalypse itself comes into view. He uses them to describe what it's like to *continue* to act when all of your actions are vain. Initially driven by the hope that his people would repent, Mormon "was forbidden to preach unto them, because of the hardness of their hearts" (Mormon 1:17). When, eventually, Mormon is finally commanded to cry repentance, he finds that his efforts are futile. "And I did cry unto this people, but it was in vain; and they did not realize that it was the Lord that had spared them, and granted unto them a chance for repentance. And behold they did harden their hearts against the Lord their God" (Mormon 3:3). Mormon cannot save them. His people refuse to be spared. They are living in denial. They don't realize what's happening. Their hearts are hardened. Their destruction is assured.

It's over.

For Mormon, though, this moment of failure is a crucial test. How does he respond to this failure? How does he respond to the end of his world and the loss of all things? How does he respond to this loss of hope for his people? How does he act, knowing that his actions are vain?

Mormon will resolutely continue to love, regardless.

Mormon exemplifies what it means to be a disciple of Christ by demonstrating *how* to sacrifice all things: he recenters his actions on the actions themselves and he willingly sacrifices his investment in the hoped for outcomes. Or, to put this more starkly: Mormon, living through the end of the world, learns how to love without, in the process, hoping that his love will prevent the world from ending. He learns to sacrifice by sacrificing any hope for gain. Sacrificing his hope that loving the Nephites would save them, he continues to love them anyway.

By loving without hope, Mormon is initiated into the "pure love of Christ" that "seeketh not her own" (Moroni 7:47; 1 Corinthians 13:5). He is initiated into a mode of action that, by sacrificing its attachment to any particular outcome, becomes incapable of failure. "Whether there be prophecies, they shall fail; whether there be tongues, they shall cease; whether there be knowledge, it shall vanish away" (1 Corinthians 13:8). If all such things are destined to fail, cease, and vanish away, why is it that, in contrast, "charity never faileth" (1 Corinthians 13:8)? Why is that, even as the world ends and all things are lost, the pure love of Christ persists? The pure love of Christ—a love purified of "hope" for gain and success— cannot fail because the work of love is its own justification. The work of love, regardless of what outcomes it generates, is always worth doing for its own sake.

As the end nears for his people, Mormon reports that he "did repent of the oath which I had made that I would no more assist them; and they gave me command again of their armies, for they looked upon me as though I could deliver them from their afflictions" (Mormon 5:1). Mormon knows, however, that he won't succeed. He knows he can't deliver them from their afflictions. He can't save them from their enemies. "But behold, I was without hope, for I knew the judgments of the Lord which should come upon them; for they repented not of their iniquities, but did struggle for their lives without calling upon that Being who created them" (Mormon 5:2). Mormon is "without hope" that his intervention will deliver his people from their afflictions. What, as a result, does he do? He intervenes anyway. He loves them and serves them and dies with them anyway. And, in this extremity, his actions throw into sharp relief the animating spirit of sacrifice that characterizes even the most ordinary gestures of love and service: good in themselves, they are done for their own sake.

Similarly, Mormon describes how, "notwithstanding their wickedness I had led them many times to battle, and had loved them, according to the love of God which was in me, with all my heart; and my soul had been poured out in prayer unto my God all the day long for them; nevertheless, it was without faith, because of the hardness of their hearts" (Mormon 3:12). Again, Mormon's description is exemplary. Notwithstanding their wickedness and their coming destruction, Mormon "loved them, according to the love of God which was in me, with all my heart" (Mormon 3:12). This love expresses itself in a specific way, through a specific form of sacrifice. As he describes it, Mormon's love expresses itself through the adoption of a sober and apocalyptic mode of Christian *action*: continual prayer. He conducts all of his actions as prayers, *as* sacrificial gestures that "poured [themselves] out in prayer unto [their] God all the day long" (Mormon 3:12). He adopts a mode of action that pours itself out without any hope of gain or success, a mode of action that pours itself out in love for a world that, perpetually created and dissolved and recreated, cannot but be lost—moment after moment, hour after hour, day after day, year after year, lifetime after lifetime, again and again. He adopts a Christ-like mode of action that, sober and attentive, is capable of simultaneously witnessing the loss of all things *and* loving those same things even as they inevitably pass away.

In this way, Mormon fleshes out the image of discipleship sketched by Paul in 1 Corinthians 7. Like Mormon, Paul understands his world's end to be nigh.

In the face of this apocalypse, he urges his fellow Christians to adopt a mode of action that both sacrifices all things and lovingly cares for them. He urges a mode of action that cares for the world *by* lovingly sacrificing the world. "The time is short," Paul writes, and given how little time is left, "it remaineth, that both they that have wives be as though they had none; and they that weep, as though they wept not; and they that rejoice, as though they rejoice not; and they that buy, as though they possessed not; and they that use this world, as not abusing it: for the fashion [i.e., the *schema* or present shape] of this world passeth away" (1 Corinthians 7:29–31). Given that the present shape of this world is passing away, we cannot act as if the world is ours to keep. Even as the world persists, we must relate to its inevitable loss by way of a preemptive sacrifice that witnesses rather than denies this loss. We must love the world as though it were already gone. We must possess the treasures we've acquired "as though [we] possessed not." We must "use this world, as not abusing it." Sheer loss bridges into redemptive sacrifice by way of this "as though." Acting as *though* the world had already ended liberates our actions from any ulterior hope for gain and, in the process, empowers our now liberated actions to care far more effectively and selflessly for the world that, for the moment, does remain.

Sacrificing all things, living as though our possessions were not our own, we become stewards rather than proprietors. We become caretakers rather than consumers. Without hope of keeping anything for ourselves, we consecrate our time, our talent, and our money—everything that we have been given or ever will be given—to the work of love. In the process, we find ourselves capable of selflessly caring for the world as it passes away and we find ourselves fitted by God's love for receiving the new worlds, now rising, that he has only begun to create.

8

Imperfections

"Now that you don't have to be perfect, you can be good."
—John Steinbeck

This passing world is not what we would like it to be. Constantly re/created by a Creator who does not cease to create (or perform miracles, or rain down revelations, or be God), we are called to love what we cannot keep, to love what defies our understanding, and to love what cannot satisfy. Undermining our hopes for satisfaction, God offers peace instead. While we can lovingly witness a kaleidoscopic succession of worlds and, thus, find peace in Christ, this peace doesn't result from acquiring or keeping treasures and satisfactions. It results, rather, from loving what we will lose. Seen from the perspective of God's eternal work of creation, this world's failures, disappointments, and imperfections shine with a different light. Shining with divine light, these imperfections are transfigured and the work of sacrificing all things shows itself clearly for what it ultimately is: the work of forgiving all things.

To sacrifice all things is to forgive all things. And to forgive all things is to perpetually forgive their inevitable passing.

This is what the damned cannot do. They cannot forgive the world's passing. They would rather live without God than without the fantasy of satisfaction. They cannot witness the world as it is. If, like the damned, we *expect* the world to be a finished product and the satisfactions that it offers to be more than fleeting, then the world will show up as full of imperfections. If we cling to the fiction of a blessedly concluded creation, polished and complete, rather than loving the ongoing process of creation itself, then the worlds and people God is now graciously re/creating will strike us as ill-formed and half-baked. Expecting a frozen perfection, we'll see only a live parade of imperfections. We'll be frustrated. We'll be disappointed. We'll despise this unfinished world and our unfinished selves. Like the damned, we'll want to curse this world and the God who un/makes it. More, we'll be moved to curse ourselves and our own passing. We'll want to bury our treasures, lock away our loved ones, and renounce the work of witnessing. Angry at the loss of all things, we'll take up our swords. We'll want revenge.

Disciples, on the contrary, practice forgiveness as a bearing. They practice forgiveness as a sober and attentive existential mood, as a posture, as a manner of life, as a way of moving through this world and steering *into* its re/creation. At the most basic level, disciples willingly participate in God's work of re/creating the world by forgiving the necessity of the world's re/creation. They sacrifice all things by withholding condemnation.

The word "imperfections" is used five times in the Book of Mormon and all of them are in Mormon 8–9. In these chapters, Moroni repeatedly uses the term to describe how he fears his future readers will react to the Book of Mormon. He fears that his readers will find the book to be imperfect, inadequate, and unsatisfying. In this respect, Moroni's counsel about how to respond to the Book of Mormon's imperfections offers a case study in how to live in a larger world that is itself imperfect and incomplete.

On Moroni's account, forgiveness empowers us to see the truth. Forgiveness opens onto a truthful witness of this world's passing. In Mormon 8, Moroni promises a gift of greater knowledge to those who resist the urge to condemn the Book of Mormon's imperfections. He promises entry into a different way of seeing and judging the world. "And whoso receiveth this record, and shall not condemn it because of the imperfections which are in it, the same shall know of greater things than these" (Mormon 8:12). If we can receive the record, witness what it offers, and withhold condemnation of its imperfections, then this witness will empower us to see even "greater things than these." Our witness will open onto a deeper, truer vision of the world that sees its imperfections as a redemptive call to create again—and love again, and sacrifice again, and create again.

To be invited into this greater knowledge is to be invited into seeing this unfinished world as the Creator does. "If there be faults they be the faults of man. But behold, we know no fault; nevertheless God knoweth all things; therefore, he that condemneth, let him be aware lest he shall be in danger of hell fire" (Mormon 8:17). In Mormon 8:12, Moroni doesn't hesitate to talk about "the imperfections" in the record. However, in Mormon 8:17, he does balk at describing these imperfections as faults: "if there be faults they be the faults of a man. But behold, we know no fault." To cross the line from seeing these imperfections with the clear and unclouded vision of a witness to deciding that these imperfections therefore deserve to be condemned as faults is to cross the line from the disciple to the damned. God is the judge, we are the witnesses. It's not our job to condemn. It's our job to love, and to love even our enemies. "Therefore, he that condemneth, let him be aware lest he shall be in danger of hell fire" (Mormon 8:17). Living as someone who curses this world and condemns its imperfections as faults rather than as occasions for healing and creation—this is itself a curse. Such is the life of the damned. To curse the loss of all things and condemn this unfinished world *is* to experience hell fire. Unable to forgive the loss of all things, the damned cannot willingly sacrifice all things. Cursing God and wishing to die, they are burned to the ground by their own maledictions. For the damned, the world's imperfections present themselves only as trouble and condemnations, never as occasions for re/creation and love.

Unable to forgive the re/creation of all things, the damned refuse to enter the presence of the Creator. They refuse to actively and willingly participate in the world's dissolution and re/creation. What would it look like, though, to live in the presence of God and willingly participate in the world's re/creation? At the conclusion of his own record, Mormon describes it plainly. Those who can forgive the loss of all things are given "to dwell in the presence of God in his kingdom, to sing ceaseless praises with the choirs above, unto the Father, and unto the Son, and unto the Holy Ghost, which are one God, in a state of happiness which hath no end" (Mormon 7:7). To live in the presence of God is to sing ceaseless praises with the choirs above. God's presence is entered by passing through this veil of gratitude. Given the loss of all things, such gratitude can be hard to muster. Ceaseless praise is hard work. It requires patience and effort. It requires care and unbroken attention. It demands the persistent and intentional cultivation of a broken heart that can swell wide as eternity.

The work of gratitude—of ceaselessly praising God in the thick of all life's troubles—is carried out by willingly returning to God everything we've been given. It's done by sacrificing all things. It's done by affirming the work of creation. Rather than condemning the world's imperfection and incompletion, we practice giving thanks to God for the privilege of witnessing and participating in that world's new creation. "Condemn me not because of mine imperfection," Moroni writes, "neither my father, because of his imperfection, neither them who have written before him; but rather *give thanks unto God* that he hath made manifest unto you our imperfections, that ye may learn to be more wise than we have been" (Mormon 9:31, emphasis added). This is the difficult path of discipleship: as the world ends and begins again—and ends and begins again—condemn not, but rather give thanks.

9

Revenge

"I will have such revenges on you both,
That all the world shall—I will do such things,—
What they are, yet I know not: but they shall be
The terrors of the earth."
—William Shakespeare, King Lear

If we cannot forgive the loss of all things, we'll be filled with fear at the thought of losing them. We'll be overwhelmed by worries and anxieties. We'll spend our lives in a defensive crouch, trying to hoard treasures and ward off re/creation. We'll waste our days clinging to pleasures that, having had a beginning, will inevitably have an end. Standing with his forces prior to their final battle at Cumorah, Mormon watches these very fears materialize before his people's eyes, personified now by the Lamanite armies. "And it came to pass that my people, with their wives and their children, did now behold the armies of the Lamanites marching towards them; and with that awful fear of death which fills the breasts of all the wicked, did they await to receive them" (Mormon 6:7). Faced with the loss of all things, an awful fear of death fills the breasts of the wicked. Mixed with the sorrowing of the damned, this cocktail of fear and sorrow clouds their vision and saps their strength. It dependably threatens to collapse into despair or harden into anger.

When this mix of fear and sorrow hardens into anger, revenge—rather than forgiveness—is the order of the day. It is his people's explicit adoption of revenge as their objective that prompts Mormon to "utterly refuse from this time forth to be a commander and a leader of this people" (Mormon 3:11). Though, "notwithstanding their wickedness [he] had led them many times to battle, and had loved them," Mormon's call to faithfully witness the end of the world bars him from accompanying his people down this dark path (Mormon 3:12). He cannot witness except by way of sacrifice and forgiveness. He will sacrifice his life in their defense but he cannot join them in their pursuit of revenge.

The Nephites, though, are ripe for this dark desire to take root in their hearts. For them, "the day of grace was passed" (Mormon 2:15). The work of creation ceased long ago. Living without God in the world, it only takes a few fortunate victories for the Nephites to turn (see Mormon 3:7–8). "And now, because of this great thing which my people, the Nephites, had done, they began to boast in their own strength, and began to swear before the heavens that they would avenge themselves of the blood of their brethren who had been slain by their enemies" (Mormon 3:9). It is no surprise that, at this moment of sworn vengeance, the Nephites begin to invoke "the heavens" again. A hallmark of vengeance is its predictable move to hijack the forms of religion and justice, only to empty these forms and repurpose them to their own retaliatory ends. Vengeance predictably and profanely "swears before the heavens" because the project of revenge is itself a way of playing God. Vengeance is a potent form of idolatry.

Mormon emphasizes this point when he explains that his people didn't just swear by the heavens, "they did swear by the heavens, and also by the throne of God, that they would go up to battle against their enemies, and would cut them off from the face of the land" (Mormon 3:10). Swearing by the throne of God, the Nephites aim to claim it as their own. They aim to depose God and occupy his throne for themselves. Their forbidden oaths dress up their anger as the divinely sanctioned prosecution of justice. Their fear of losing everything authorizes them, in the name of revenge, to do anything. By invoking God's throne, they hope to commandeer religion, jettison the profoundly troubling commandment to sacrifice all things, and substitute for sacrifice the pseudo-religious work of making sure, in God's own name, that people finally get what they deserve.

God's response to these oaths of vengeance is emphatic and uncompromising: vengeance is never ours. In the span of Mormon's nine chapters, both Mormon and Moroni echo Paul's version of Deuteronomy 32:35 as we have it in Romans 12:19. Mormon recounts how, "when they had sworn by all that had been forbidden them by our Lord and Savior Jesus Christ, that they would go up unto their enemies to battle, and avenge themselves of the blood of their brethren, behold the voice of the Lord came unto me, saying: Vengeance is mine, and I will repay; and because this people repented not after I had delivered them, behold, they shall be cut off from the face of the earth" (Mormon 3:14–15). Vengeance, if it is to be executed, is the sole province of the Lord. Moroni repeats the same claim in Mormon 8:20: "Behold what the scripture says—man shall not smite, neither shall he judge; for judgment is mine, saith the Lord, and vengeance is mine also, and I will repay."

However, despite marking vengeance as a work that belongs exclusively to God, there are good reasons to think that God himself is not in the business of revenge. In fact, as I'll argue in the next chapter, there are good reasons to think that God is not even in the business of making sure that people get what they deserve. If we find, as Moroni warns, that "the sword of vengeance hangeth over [us]," this isn't because God endorses that vengeance but because, refusing to sacrifice, we've willed it upon ourselves (Mormon 8:41). With our fists clenched and our hearts set on revenge, we won't accept anything less. The sword of vengeance hangs over those who insist on drawing that sword. Or, at least, the loss of all things inevitably shows up for the wicked as an act of vengeance because they refuse to join God in willing the re/creation of the world. The day of grace—of creation and recreation—arrives for the damned as a curse. With God at the wheel, the sun is set to rise on a new world and, like it or not, the old world will be swept away "even as a dew before the sun" (Mormon 4:18).

The damned, though, won't have it. Instead, they deny the ongoing reality of God's creative work and "breathe out wrath and strifes against the work of the Lord" (Mormon 8:21). "We will destroy the work of the Lord," they tell themselves (Mormon 8:21). This wrath, though, is futile. "Who can stand against the works of the Lord? . . . Who will *despise* the works of the Lord? Who will despise the children of Christ? Behold, all ye who are despisers of the works of the Lord, for ye shall wonder and perish" (Mormon 9:26, emphasis added).

The damned will wonder and perish because, despite their curses and oaths, "the eternal purposes of the Lord shall roll on" (Mormon 8:22).

Enmeshed in this world's continual re/creation, there is only one path forward. We must give up on revenge. We must stop cursing and despising. We must stop playing God. We must sacrifice all things by forgiving all things. We must "lay down [our] weapons of war, and delight no more in the shedding of blood" (Mormon 7:4).

10

Getting Gain

*"Truly I am Mahan, the master of this great secret,
that I may murder and get gain."* —Moses 5:31

The damned don't just break ranks with religion, they
co-opt it. They hijack it. This is crucial to see. As I
argued in chapter seven, if sin is the business of living in denial—of denying that God is God in a bid to
install oneself as god, a god fully empowered to pass
judgment on and refuse the world's re/creation—then
sin isn't just going to involve breaking God's law. It
isn't just going to involve abandoning religion. If sin
is the business of playing God, then sin will also (inevitably) be the business of playing at religion. Sin will
always build up churches unto itself. Like a parasite,
sin will attach itself to the host of a true religion and
slowly but steadily repurpose that tradition's scrip-
tures, rituals, and communities to its own bitter ends.

What does a hijacked religion look like? To what
ends is God's law repurposed by sin? Moroni is
clear about the answer to this question. Where God
intends religion to function as a framework for collectively sacrificing all things, sin repurposes religion
as an apparatus for "getting gain." As sinners, we
have "built up churches unto [ourselves] to get gain"
(Mormon 8:33). Ironically, this fixation on getting
gain and avoiding sacrifice is also what forecloses the
possibility of real prosperity. Refusing the world's re/
creation, we refuse the divine prosperity that can only
emerge from a willingly renewed world.

The darkest example of this parody of true religion comes bundled with Mormon's horrific report that, after gaining the city Teancum, the Lamanite armies "did drive the inhabitants forth out of her, and did take many prisoners both women and children, and did offer them up as sacrifices unto their idol gods" (Mormon 4:14). When the Lamanites subsequently attack the city Boaz, the same horror repeats itself. Initially repulsed, the Lamanites overrun the city on their second try and "the Nephites were driven and slaughtered with an exceedingly great slaughter; their women and their children were again sacrificed unto idols" (Mormon 4:21). This is idolatry at its most stark and brutal. Idolaters, understanding religion as the business of getting gain, repurpose the forms of sacrifice for the sake of entering into a *quid pro quo* with their idolatrous gods. Each time they are rewarded with success, each time they gain from their idols the treasure they desire, they offer sacrifices in return. Living without God in the world, they (unlike Mormon) live *with* the firm hope that life can be lived as the acquisition of all things. Their hearts are fixed on winning. And their idols, as projections of their own fantasies of control and satisfaction, will help them win. Rather than continually sacrificing all things as though these things had already been lost, they repurpose religion as the work of sacrificing just *some* few things in the hope that they will thereby get gain. They ironically repurpose sacrifice as a way of avoiding the necessity of sacrificing of all things.

Moroni offers a similar description of how, in the latter-days, churches will operate for the sake of gain. "Behold I say unto you," Moroni begins, "that those saints who have gone before me, who have possessed this land, shall cry, yea, even from the dust will they cry" (Mormon 8:23). When that day comes and these lost voices are heard once more, we will know that the end of the world is near. "It shall come in a day when there shall be heard of fires, and tempests, and vapors of smoke in foreign lands; and there shall also be heard of wars, rumors of wars, and earthquakes in divers places. Yea, it shall come in a day when there shall be great pollutions upon the face of the earth" (Mormon 8:29–31). As the world ends, religion will get repurposed as an escape plan, as an insurance policy against the necessity of losing all things. It will promise to spare us the work of sacrifice and liberate us from the work of possessing as though we possessed not. "It shall come in a day," Moroni says, "when there shall be churches built up that shall say: Come unto me, and for your money you shall be forgiven of your sins" (Mormon 8:32). These are what the last days look like. In return for money, sins can be forgiven. In return for money, our sinful refusals and denials can be ratified and sanctified by religion itself.

Ultimately, however, such reassuring denials of the world's dissolution only have the power to ratify our own damnation. "O ye wicked and perverse and stiff-necked people, why have ye built up churches unto yourselves to get gain? Why have ye transfigured the holy word of God, that ye might bring damnation upon your souls" (Mormon 8:33)? Or again: "why do ye build up your secret abominations to get gain" (Mormon 8:40)? The central problem here, as Moroni so incisively puts it, is that our desire to avoid sacrifice and get gain *transfigures* the holy word of God. The damned don't just attack or renounce the word of God, they transfigure it.

Sin bends God's words into new shapes by pitching those words as answers to its own errant questions. Swapping out parts, sin repositions God's law as a useful widget in its own engine of refusal and denial. Burdened with the work of cursing the world and despising the costs of re/creation, sin commandeers God's law as a tool for justifying and amplifying those curses. In the hands of the damned, the point of God's law is not love and sacrifice. The point of God's law is to curse and condemn. The point of the law is revenge. Or, perhaps most succinctly, the point of the law is to make sure that people finally get what they *deserve*.

When, in the end, "your souls are racked with a consciousness of guilt," Moroni asks, will you finally understand "that ye have ever abused his laws" (Mormon 9:3)? This, on my view, is what defines a sinful transfiguration of God's law. The law is transfigured by sin when it is *abused* and it is abused when it is used as a means to get gain. The law is abused when it is used to answer the question: what is deserved? The law is abused when it is used to divide the world into despised losers (who lose everything) and imaginary winners (who get gain and, therefore, momentarily appear to magically avoid the loss of everything). Then, to top off this abuse, the damned use the idea of God to rubberstamp the labels and curses they've awarded. They dole out these labels and curses on the basis of what they think is deserved and they decide what is deserved on the basis of the treasures and successes each person gained (or failed to gain) through their hijacked version of the law. Given the importance of these treasures and successes to religion as a means of getting gain, it should be obvious, then, why an abuse of the law goes hand in hand with a fixation on wealth as a pseudo-sign of divine favor:

> Behold, I speak unto you as if ye were present, and yet ye are not. But behold, Jesus Christ hath shown you unto me, and I know your doing. And I know that ye do walk in the pride

of your hearts; and there are none save a few
only who do not lift themselves up in the pride
of their hearts, unto the wearing of very fine
apparel, unto envying, and strifes, and malice,
and persecutions, and all manner of iniquities; and your churches, yea, even every one,
have become polluted because of the pride of
your hearts. For behold, ye do love money, and
your substance, and your fine apparel, and the
adorning of your churches, more than ye love
the poor and the needy, the sick and the afflicted. (Mormon 8:35–37)

Here, the wicked take the mark of a successful religious
gesture to be the possibility of avoiding the loss of all
things. The mark of a successful sacrifice is getting gain.
Or, at least, the mark of a successful sacrifice is getting
enough gain to temporarily disguise the inevitable loss
of all things. Those who *are* visibly losing all things—the
poor, the needy, the sick, the afflicted—are understood
by the damned to *deserve* whatever losses they suffer. If
a beggar puts up his petition to them, the damned will
say to themselves: this "man has brought upon himself
his misery; therefore I will stay my hand, and will not
give unto him of my food, nor impart unto him of my
substance that he may not suffer, for his punishments
are just" (Mosiah 4:17). The damned use the law as justification for despising and cursing. They abuse the law
to avoid what they themselves fear most: sickness, poverty, old age, and death. If beggars suffer, the damned
think, they must deserve their suffering. If the wealthy
are comfortable, they must deserve their comfort. The
point of religion is, in either case, to endorse these idolatrous fantasies of "just" desserts with magical thinking
and talismanic trophies.

This, however, is not what it looks like to serve the true and living God. The disciple, soberly witnessing the end of the world, isn't afraid of the world's creation, dissolution, and recreation. The disciple isn't afraid of sickness, poverty, old age, or death. The disciple, living through the end of the world and loving without hope of gain, stands "with a firmness unshaken" in Christ and responds to the beggar's petition with grace and generosity (Mormon 9:28). "Ask not," Moroni counsels, "that ye may consume it on your lusts, but ask with a firmness unshaken, that ye will yield to no temptation, but that ye will serve the true and living God" (Mormon 9:28). The temptation is always the same: to run from the true and living Creator. The temptation is to live in denial. The disciple, rather than running, stands firm. Rather than abusing the law for the sake of consumption, the disciple sacrifices by way of the law in order to participate in the world's re/creation.

Emulating their master, disciples of Christ use the law to judge the answer to a very different kind of question. Rather than asking: what is deserved? The disciple asks: what is needed? When, in the Sermon on the Mount, Christ counsels us to "judge not, that ye be not judged," he is referring to this first, abusive use of the law (Matthew 7:1). When, as the Joseph Smith

Translation has it, Christ urges us to instead "judge not unrighteously, that ye be not judged; but judge righteous judgment," he is referring to this second form of judgment (Matthew 7:1–2, JST). What does it mean to abuse the law and judge unrighteously? It means to use the law to judge what is *deserved*. What, on the contrary, does it mean to use the law to judge righteously? It means to use the law to judge what, in the face of the world's continual re/creation, is *needed*.

What, given the loss of all things, is needed? The answer to this question is clear enough. Discipleship is needed. Disciples covenant "to bear one another's burdens, that they may be light" (Mosiah 18:8). They covenant to "mourn with those that mourn; yea, and comfort those that stand in need of comfort, and to stand as witnesses of God at all times and in all things, and in all places that ye may be in, even until death, that ye may be redeemed of God" (Mosiah 18:9). Disciples, like Mormon, are called to stand as sober witnesses, at all times and in all places, as God continues to un/make the world. They are called, standing amid this un/making, to mourn with those that mourn and comfort those that stand in need of comfort. They are called, in short, to love the world and fulfill the law by sacrificing all things.

Mormon 6:

8. And it came to pass that they came to battle against us, and every soul was filled with terror because of the greatness of their numbers.

9. And it came to pass that they did fall upon my people with the sword, and with the bow, and with the arrow, and with the ax, and with all manner of weapons of war.

10 And it came to pass that my men were hewn down, yea, even my ten thousand who were with me, and I fell wounded in the midst; and they passed by me that they did not put an end to my life.

11 And when they had gone through and hewn down all my people save it were twenty and four of us, (among whom was my son Moroni) and we having survived the dead of our people, did behold on the morrow, when the Lamanites had returned unto their camps, from the top of the hill Cumorah, the ten thousand of my people who were hewn down, being led in the front by me.

12. And we also beheld the ten thousand of my people who were led by my son Moroni.

13. And behold the ten thousand of Gigiddonah had fallen, and he also in the midst.

14. And Lamah had fallen with his ten thousand;

and Gilgal had fallen with his
ten thousand;

and Limhah had fallen with his
ten thousand;

and Jeneum had fallen with his
ten thousand;

and Cumenihah,
and Moronihah,
and Antionum,
and Shiblom,
and Shem,
and Josh,
had fallen with
their ten thousand each.

15. And it came to pass that there were ten more who did fall by the sword, with their ten thousand each;

yea, even all my people, save it were those twenty and four who were with me,

and also a few who had escaped into
the south countries,
and a few who had
deserted over unto the
Lamanites, had fallen;
and their flesh, and bones, and blood lay
upon the face of the earth,

being left by the hands of those who slew
them to molder upon the land, and to
crumble and to return to their mother earth.

16. And my soul was rent with anguish, because of the slain of my people, and I cried:

17. O ye fair ones, how could ye have departed from the ways of the Lord! O ye fair ones, how could ye have rejected that Jesus, who stood with open arms to receive you!

18. Behold, if ye had not done this, ye would not have fallen. But behold, ye are fallen, and I mourn your loss.

19. O ye fair sons and daughters, ye fathers and mothers, ye husbands and wives, ye fair ones, how is it that ye could have fallen!

20. But behold, ye are gone, and my sorrows cannot bring your return.

21. And the day soon cometh that your mortal must put on immortality, and these bodies which are now moldering in corruption must soon become incorruptible bodies; and then ye must stand before the judgment-seat of Christ, to be judged according to your works; and if it so be that ye are righteous, then are ye blessed with your fathers who have gone before you.

22. O that ye had repented before this great destruction had come upon you. But behold, ye are gone, and the Father, yea, the Eternal Father of heaven, knoweth your state; and he doeth with you according to his justice and mercy.

11

Judgment

"Whence things have their origin, there they must also pass away according to necessity; for they must pay penalty and be judged for their injustice, according to the ordinance of time." —Anaximander of Miletus

Living through the end of the world, we arrive at judgment day. We arrive at what Moroni calls "the day of your visitation" (Mormon 9:2). As the world ends, we're visited by the Lord. We're conducted into the presence of the Creator. We undergo—willingly or not—a new creation. To willingly undergo that re/creation is to be saved. To unwillingly undergo that re/creation is to be damned. Either way, the world will end, judgment will be rendered, and a new world will begin. Judgment day, in this respect, is the hinge on which a new creation turns. It ushers us into this new world. Taking stock of creation, God judges what is needed in order to end the old world and make it new.

What is needed in order to end the old world and make it new? Sacrifice. The old world must be sacrificed in order to make the new world. The work of re/creating all things is the work of sacrificing all things. God cannot judge the world and inaugurate a new creation if creation itself stubbornly clings to its past, refusing to sacrifice itself. He cannot inaugurate a new creation if everything about this new creation is decided, lockstep, by what has already happened. The function of God's law is not to lock the world into following its current course, dictating future consequences solely on the basis of past actions. Far from enacting justice, this sort of lockstep fantasy is just another way of sinfully denying that there *will* be a new world: we imagine up unto ourselves a future wholly owned by the past, captured and predictable and sequestered like a treasure safely buried in the earth. As sinners, we defensively imagine the world to be unchangeable, unsaveable, unrecreatable. We imagine the future to be predetermined, we paint agency as a fiction, and, parodically, we envision justice as the execution of this predetermination. But this is not the case. The function of God's law is not to predetermine the future on the basis of the past and, thus, prevent the world's re/creation. The function of God's law doesn't align with our sinful denials. The function of God's law is to guide us (again and again) through the world's dissolution and re/creation. The function of God's law is to teach us how to participate in the world's re/creation by teaching us how to sacrifice all things.

On judgment day the law will be fulfilled and justice will flood the earth. But such justice won't arrive as a preprogrammed consequence fixed by the past. This justice will arrive, instead, as a break with the old world of sin. It will arrive as an integral part of what it means for the world to finally be made new in love.

As a result, justice is poorly defined as the backward-looking business of making sure that people get what they "deserve." Justice isn't a form of religiously sanctioned vengeance. It isn't a form of revenge dressed up as a divinely endorsed system of prizes and punishments that carves the world up into winners and losers. Certainly, this way of thinking about justice comes naturally to us—we want gain and we want revenge. And certainly, forbidden to exercise vengeance on our own behalf, we naturally gravitate toward the fantasy that, ultimately, an all-powerful God will inflict an all-power-ful vengeance for us.

But this way of thinking about justice is a poor fit for a just God bent on creating a new world. It's a poor fit for a just God who loves his enemies. It's a poor fit for a just God who personally sacrifices all things in unforced and self-emptying acts of love that are anything but pre-determined by the past. Similarly, Mormon and Moroni both strain against these natural assumptions about justice. Their way of talking about judgment repeatedly calls into question any link between justice and ven-geance. Instead, they push us toward a model of justice that is grounded in sacrifice and re/creation rather than in blind, mechanical consequence.

Mormon, for one, is clear that the damned *will* find themselves punished on judgment day. They will be punished as the world ends and, with a gnashing of teeth, they will lose all things. But Mormon also argues that God will not do the punishing. At its most imme-diate, this punishment for the wicked is doled out by the wicked themselves. "The judgments of God will overtake the wicked," Mormon claims, but "it is by the wicked that the wicked are punished; for it is the wicked that stir up the hearts of the children of men unto blood-shed" (Mormon 4:5). The wicked punish the wicked. Or, as Moroni even more pointedly puts it, this sort of pun-ishment is not only doled out by the wicked themselves, it is doled out by the wicked *upon* themselves.

> Behold, will ye believe in the day of your visita-tion?...Do ye suppose that ye shall dwell with him under a consciousness of your guilt? Do ye suppose that ye could be happy to dwell with that holy Being, when your souls are racked with a consciousness of guilt that ye have ever abused his laws? Behold, I say unto you that

ye would be more miserable to dwell with a holy and just God, under a consciousness of your filthiness before him, than ye would to dwell with the damned souls in hell. For behold, when ye shall be brought to see your nakedness before God, and also the glory of God, and the holiness of Jesus Christ, it will kindle a flame of unquenchable fire upon you. (Mormon 9:2–5)

What kindles a flame of unquenchable fire in the souls of the damned? A consciousness—a witness—of the fact that, having lost all things, they stand naked in the presence of God. Stripped of their treasures and jewelry and fine apparel, naked and defenseless before the glory of the Creator, caught in the fire of the world's continual re/creation, the damned yearn to banish themselves from the presence of God. If we find ourselves in this position, "we shall not dare to look up to our God; and we would fain be glad if we could command the rocks and the mountains to fall upon us to hide us from his presence" (Alma 12:14). By abusing God's law and refusing to sacrifice all things, the damned condemn themselves to the unmitigated loss of all things.

If the damned punish themselves, if they invariably experience the loss of all things as a punishment, then how ought we to read passages like the following that, in Moroni's own words, describe this judgment as a frozen, final state imposed by God? "And then cometh the judgment of the Holy One upon them; and then cometh the time that he that is filthy shall be filthy still; and he that is righteous shall be righteous still; he that is happy shall be happy still; and he that is unhappy shall be unhappy still" (Mormon 9:14). Here, the day of judgment is described as the moment when creation is arrested and the world receives its final, finished form. Once judgment has been rendered, the filthy will stay filthy and the righteous will stay righteous.

How we interpret passages like this will depend on context. In particular, their interpretation will depend on the breadth and depth of the context we use to frame our questions about them. If we hold that God creates only occasionally—if his commitment to the ongoing work of creation is not understood to be very thing that causes God to be God—and we then narrowly limit the scope of that creative work to just one world on one former occasion, then this more customary way of talking makes sense. But if, with a wider view, we understand creation itself as the ongoing miracle at the heart of God's divine work, if we understand that work to be not only past tense but ongoing, and if we understand that work to apply not only to this world but to worlds without number, then we'll need a different approach. Rather than bringing this one world to a permanent end, the day of judgment would need to be understood as that which permanently imposes God's work of continually creating, dissolving, and recreating the world. And in that case, the necessity of continually responding to this permanent reality—either with a desire for revenge or a willingness to sacrifice—will itself be permanent.

The reality of the world's continual re/creation is not going to change. God is not going to stop creating. Time will continue to flow. This world will never cease to pass away and new worlds will never cease to roll into being. Progression is eternal. And, as a result, love's work is itself never ending.

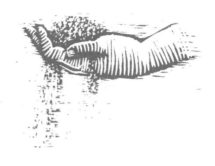

12

The Lamb of God

"We go from day to day, one day much like the next, and then on a certain day all unannounced we come upon a man... who makes a certain gesture of himself that is like the piling of one's goods upon an altar and in this gesture we recognize that which is buried in our hearts and is never truly lost to us nor ever can be." —*Cormac McCarthy*

But what about justice? What happens when justice is no longer defined as the backward-looking business of making sure that people get only what they deserve on the basis of what they've done in the past? What happens when God's law and the justice it enables are no longer hijacked by the damned as reactionary bulwarks against the work of re/creation? What happens when justice is uncoupled from revenge? What happens when justice is, instead, recognized as an integral, forward-looking part of creating a *new* world?

What happens then? Justice.

The work of justice is inseparable from God in the same way that the miraculous work of creation is inseparable from God. If the miraculous work of creation ceased, God "would cease to be God" (Mormon 9:19–20). And, similarly: "the work of justice could not be destroyed; if so, God would cease to be God" (Alma 42:13). Here, the work of justice and the work of re/creation bleed into one another as two aspects of the same work of love. The creation of a just world is inseparable from what it means for a new world to be re/created in

God's image. To this end, God puts his laws to work in the service of love in order to judge what is needed rather than what is deserved.

God's law is an indispensable outline of what, at any given moment, is needed. It shows us how to act, how to think, how to obey, and how to love. In particular, as an indispensable set of instructions for how to sacrifice all things, the law is crucial to re/creating the world in the image of God. The law bears the image of God because it shows us how to sacrifice *like* God. It shows us how to do what God does. It shows us how to participate in the re/creation of all things by willingly sacrificing all things.

In the end, this is what must be witnessed: that God himself is not exempt from the work of sacrificing all things. There is no alternate path. There are no shortcuts. Mormon intends his own witness to serve this purpose. "I write unto you," he says, "that ye may know that ye must all stand before the judgment-seat of Christ," and so that you may know that there are "other witness besides him whom they saw and heard, that Jesus, whom they slew, was the very Christ and the very God" (Mormon 3:20–21). Incredible as it may sound to the damned, the very Christ—in fact, "the very God"—is the one who willingly lost all things, including his own life, to re/create both himself and the world. Mormon repeats this idea again in chapter 7 at the heart of his final set of exhortations: "Believe in Jesus Christ, that he is the Son of God, and that he was slain by the Jews, and by the power of the Father he hath risen again, whereby he hath gained the victory over the grave; and also in him is the sting of death swallowed up" (Mormon 7:5). If you plan to worship God, if you hope to be re/created in the image of God, this is the God you must worship: a God in whom the sting of death is thankfully swallowed up, but a God who, *nonetheless*, had to willingly pass through death's door himself.

Moroni adds his own witness to this same effect. In order to no "longer deny the Christ," Moroni writes, we must learn how to "behold the Lamb of God" (Mormon 9:3). We must stop covering our eyes and hiding our heads in the sand, repeating the mantra that "all is well in Zion" (2 Nephi 28:21). We must stop pretending that there is any other way to pass through the crucible of this world's continual re/creation than by following the sacrificial example of "the Lamb."

> And now, I speak also concerning those who do not believe in Christ. Behold, will ye believe in the day of your visitation—behold, when the Lord shall come, yea, even that great day when the earth shall be rolled together as a scroll, and the elements shall melt with fervent heat, yea, in that great day when ye shall be brought to stand before the Lamb of God— then will ye say that there is no God? Then will ye longer deny the Christ, or can ye behold the Lamb of God? (Mormon 9:1–3)

Witnessing the world's end, watching as the elements melt with fervent heart, will we continue to deny that Christ is God? Will we continue to worship some other (much safer) God than the continual Creator? Will we continue to pretend that the law could be fulfilled (even hypothetically) in some way other than by the sacrificial blood of the Lamb? Will we continue to pretend that the law, repurposed for the sake getting gain (spiritual or physical), could be used to avoid the necessity of sacrificing all things? Will we continue to pretend that the law could be fulfilled in some way other than by love? Or that love itself could be accomplished in some way other than by sacrifice? Will we continue to pretend that it's possible to enact justice and fulfill the law without love?

How is justice achieved? *Only by fulfilling the law.*

How is the law fulfilled? *Only by way of love.*

How is love enacted? *Only by way of sacrifice.*

Atoning sacrifice isn't simply what is required after the fact, as a kind of cosmic band-aid, because the law—which wouldn't have needed sacrifice otherwise— was broken. God's own atoning act of sacrifice wasn't the backup plan. Rather, because the law can only *ever* be fulfilled by way of love and sacrifice, the whole plan of redemption works the other way around: the fantasy that sacrifice is avoidable (even by God) is what broke the law in the first place.

When asked to summarize the whole of the law in just two commandments, Christ doesn't hesitate. "Master, which is the great commandment in the law? Jesus said unto him, Thou shalt love the Lord thy God with all thy heart, and with all thy soul, and with all thy mind. This is the first and great commandment. And the second is like unto it, Thou shalt love thy neighbour as thyself. On these two commandments hang all the law and the prophets" (Matthew 22:36–40). Everything hangs on the work of love. The law itself hangs on the work of love. The law cannot be fulfilled but by way of love and love is enacted only by sacrificing all of the heart, all of the soul, and all of the mind.

Love, with clear eyes and a full heart, witnesses what is needed. Then, guided by the law, love fulfills the law by sacrificing what is needed. There is no justice if the law goes unfulfilled and the law cannot be fulfilled except by way of love. Which, of course, is just another way of saying that justice never was about deciding who deserved what. Justice, in the hands of God, fulfills the law only by answering the question:

what is needed? The law is fulfilled by asking: what, on this occasion, is needed to re/create the world as a just world? If hard consequences are needed to express love and fulfill the law, then love enforces hard consequences—but as a form of grace, not as an act of revenge. And if, instead, mercy and tenderness are needed to express love and fulfill the law, then mercy and grace are given. In either case, the law is fulfilled and it is fulfilled by love.

Justice is inseparable from love. And, conversely, there is no love without the law. But using the law to answer any other sort of question than what is needed—in particular, using the law to decide what is deserved—voids the law and empties it of force. A world in which the law is used to determine what is deserved is effectively a lawless world. It is a world ruled over by an idol rather than God. It is a world in which the law's sole, fulfilling purpose has been rendered moot. The law, obeyed for the sake of gain, is an empty gesture, divorced from its governing end. Only love can redeem what is passing away. Uncoupled from the work of sacrifice, the law is a host for sin. Uncoupled from the work of judging in righteous judgment what is needed, the law is a sinful exercise in self-congratulatory denial.

This, on my reading, is the central issue at stake in Christ's mortal ministry. Everywhere he goes, Christ finds crowds who expect him to use the law to decide what is deserved. He finds a nation waiting for a Messiah who will exact revenge. And when, instead, Christ uses the law to decide what sacrifice is needed, the people are shocked and their religious leaders are offended. Appalled, they see Christ as destroying the law, while Christ, in turn, is roused to wrath by how they abuse the law to decide what is deserved and, thus, ironically *prevent* the law from being fulfilled.

We might, in fact, take this dueling pair of questions as a template for reading the Gospels as a whole. Every time Jesus has an argument with his contemporaries, ask: who in this story is using the law to answer which question? Who is using the law to decide what is deserved? And who is using the law, on the contrary, to decide what is needed? Who is using the law to judge? And who, by way of the law, is judging righteous judgment? Who, by uncoupling the law from its end in love, is preventing the fulfillment of the law and aborting justice? And who is enacting justice by way of a loving sacrifice that is itself commanded and defined by the law?

On my reading, Christ's parables, in particular, are designed to introduce the "kingdom of God" by drawing this contrast. In the parable of the Good Samaritan, the Samaritan doesn't ask what the injured man deserves. He only asks what the injured man needs. In the parable of the Prodigal Son, the father doesn't ask what his wayward son deserves. He only asks what his wayward son needs (And the elder son is flummoxed by his father's actions because, on the contrary, he *expects* his father to use the law to decide what his prodigal brother deserves). In both cases, the answer to the question of what is needed is guided and defined by the law. And the law, in turn, is fulfilled by offering whatever sacrifices those needs call forth.

This shift in the use of the law may be most sharply illustrated in the parable of the laborers—a parable that, as long as we think of the law as a tool that *could* be uncoupled from love and used to decide what is deserved, can only confuse and frustrate us. What is the kingdom of heaven like? What does it look like when the law is fulfilled? Jesus says:

> For the kingdom of heaven is like unto a man
> that is an householder, which went out early in

the morning to hire labourers into his vineyard. And when he had agreed with the labourers for a penny a day, he sent them into his vineyard. And he went out about the third hour, and saw others standing idle in the marketplace, And said unto them; Go ye also into the vineyard, and whatsoever is right I will give you. And they went their way. Again he went out about the sixth and ninth hour, and did likewise. And about the eleventh hour he went out, and found others standing idle, and saith unto them, Why stand ye here all the day idle? They say unto him, Because no man hath hired us. He saith unto them, Go ye also into the vineyard; and whatsoever is right, that shall ye receive. So when even was come, the lord of the vineyard saith unto his steward, Call the labourers, and give them their hire, beginning from the last unto the first. And when they came that were hired about the eleventh hour, they received every man a penny. But when the first came, they supposed that they should have received more; and they likewise received every man a penny. And when they had received it, they murmured against the goodman of the house, Saying, These last have wrought but one hour, and thou hast made them equal unto us, which have borne the burden and heat of the day. But he answered one of them, and said, Friend, I do thee no wrong: didst not thou agree with me for a penny? Take that thine is, and go thy way: I will give unto this last, even as unto thee. Is it not lawful for me to do what I will with mine own? Is thine eye evil, because I am good? So the last shall be first, and the first last: for many be called, but few chosen. (Matthew 20:1–16)

The master is accused of wrongdoing. He is accused of breaking the law and leaving it unfulfilled. And if the point of the law is to make sure that each person only gets exactly what they deserve and no more, then the master's disgruntled accusers are right. Justice has been denied. It doesn't make sense for those who worked only part of the day to be given the same sum as those who labored through the whole heat of that day.

But the master's accusers are wrong. They've misunderstood the law and they've misunderstood how to fulfill it. They've misunderstood justice. In the hands of the master, the law hasn't been broken, it's been fulfilled. "Friend," the master says, "I do thee no wrong....Is it not lawful for me to do what I will with mine own? Is thine eye evil, because I am good?" The laborers are rebuked and that rebuke extends to us as well: "Is thine eye evil, because I am good?" Are we using the law to evil ends? Are we incapable of seeing the good wrought by the master as a fulfillment of the law and an execution of justice? In the hands of the master, the law is not used to make sure that people get only what they deserve. In the hands of the master, the law is fulfilled, instead, by determining what each laborer needs. And what each laborer needs is enough of a wage to stave off starvation for another day. What they need is enough daily bread to see the world re/created again tomorrow.

The master's choices, here, don't amount to a gratuitous act of mercy that flouts fulfillment of the law and compromises justice. (Such a thing would only be the case if the fulfillment of the law—and thus justice—were somehow separable from the work of love and sacrifice.) The master's actions, rather, are the

113

only sort of actions that *are* just and the only sorts of action that *could* fulfill the law. The master, guided by the law, sacrifices all things in order to meet the needs of the laborers. In the hands of the master, the ideal end represented by the law is not used to make sure that people, having fallen short of that ideal, get the vengeful punishment they deserve. In the hands of the master, justice is accomplished, instead, by using the law to determine what each person now needs in order to *approach* that ideal and embody it.

Trading our own questions about gain for God's questions about sacrifice, our values undergo a profound revaluation. We experience a mighty change of heart. We become capable of fulfilling the law. Moroni sketches this revaluation of values when, discussing the prophetic witness recorded on the plates, he draws a fine—but deep and clear—line between "gain" and "worth." Moroni claims that

> the plates thereof are of no worth, because of the commandment of the Lord. For he truly saith that no one shall have them to get gain; but the record thereof is of great worth; and whoso shall bring it to light, him will the Lord bless. For none can have power to bring it to light save it be given him of God; for God wills that it shall be done with an eye single to his glory, or the welfare of the ancient and long dispersed covenant people of the Lord. (Mormon 8:14–15)

The plates, Moroni argues, cannot be treated as treasure. "No one shall have them to get gain." And the same is true of the law: it cannot be used to get gain. But still, Moroni claims, "the record thereof *is* of great worth." While the plates cannot be used to get gain, they are of great worth. They are of great worth in educating anyone who wants to fulfill the law by way of sacrifice. The law is of enormous value to those who stop trying to leverage their obedience as collateral against the loss of all things and, instead, enter through the strait gate of sacrifice.

These competing values of "gain" and "worth" are mutually exclusive. We can measure the world in terms of its potential for gain or we can witness the world in light of its worth, but we cannot see both at the same time. To have our values revalued is to undergo a fundamental change in our bearing that attunes us to the world's worth. As long as we continue to abuse the law as a measure for what is deserved and look at the world through the lens of gain, we will never witness the world's worth. Only the work of sacrificing all things can, by way of the law, bring that worth into focus. Just as using the law to judge what is deserved voids the law and results in a lawless antinomianism, seeing the world in terms of gain conceals the world's worth and results in an idolatrous nihilism. If we cling to the world, hoping to prevent its passing, only worthless ashes will remain. If, instead, we willingly let the world pass and practice the loss of all things as a form of sacrifice, then the world's worth will shine with glory.

This is what it means, as Moroni describes it, to view the world "with an eye single to his glory" (Mormon 8:15). This is what is needed to see the world's worth. Witnessing God at work in the world's re/creation, we see his glory revealed in the world. Sacrificing our own point of view, our eye becomes single with his. And seeing the world through God's eyes, we discover—independent of gain—what is of great worth. Rather than hiding behind our attachment to created things, we learn to participate in God's work of re/creating them.

Conclusion

"We cannot be deaf to the question: 'Do I love this world so well that I have to know how it ends?'"—W.H. Auden

At the outset of this study, I defined its relatively narrow parameters. Treating history and doctrine as raw materials rather than as ends in themselves, my aims were explicitly theological. Though working with an ancient text, my intention was to think in the present tense. And, perhaps surprisingly, my theological ambitions were resolutely practical as I insisted on the priority of just one live question: exactly how, in Christ, are we saved?

To this end, I proposed to read Mormon's book as a beginner's guide to the end of the world. I proposed to read Mormon as a case study in apocalyptic discipleship and my reading was shaped throughout by a wager that the extremity of Mormon's apocalyptic discipleship could bring more clearly into view the fact that living through the end of the world (on any number of scales) is *the* fundamental framework for Christian discipleship of any kind—by anyone, in any world, in any age.

If this is true and Mormon's life can be read as an exemplary case of discipleship, then what aspects of discipleship have now been thrown into sharp relief? If, tomorrow, I want to begin again, live as a disciple of Christ, and learn how to willingly participate in the re/creation of the world, what should I do? What does this work look like? What can we conclude?

Of all that might be said, I want to focus on just two pairs of conclusions.

The first set of conclusions is largely conceptual. Together, they frame a pair of crucial conditions for *thinking* about our redemption in Christ.

(1) We should avoid thinking about justice as if it were—even theoretically—opposed to or separable from God's work of love. As a result, I take any notion of justice that does not understand love to be the governing end of God's law to be inadequately conceived and, even, morally compromised. It is never morally legitimate to use the law to get revenge, secure treasures, or avoid the end of the world. The law's only possible fulfillment is love.

(2) We should avoid thinking about love as if it were separable from justice. As a result, any approach that separates love from the work of fulfilling God's law—and, thus, from the work of sacrificing all things—is inadequately conceived and, even, morally compromised. The law, while never sufficient, is always necessary for love. Love and justice, joined in the work of judging what is needed in order to re/create the world in God's image, are never at cross-purposes.

Both of these conclusions steer us away from relying too heavily on models of redemption that, even implicitly, understand justice, law, or love to center on the work of making sure that any one of us gets what we deserve.

My second pair of conclusions is more pragmatic. Together, these conclusions frame crucial conditions for *living* as a disciple of Christ.

(1) We should avoid relying too heavily on models of discipleship that fail to foreground God's ongoing work of re/creation as the essential context for addressing sin, fulfilling God's law, and sacrificing all things. To understand the atonement, we must understand the fall, and to understand the fall, we must understand creation. True discipleship depends on a fearless commitment to witnessing this world's continual un/making. A new life in Christ begins only when we have the courage to witness (again and again) the end of the world.

(2) We should avoid relying too heavily on models of discipleship that are not grounded in the practical, difficult, and daily work of forgiving this world's continual passing. To practice discipleship is to witness (again and again) the end of the world. To practice discipleship is to transfigure the loss of all things by sacrificing all things. And to willingly sacrifice all things is to willingly forgive all things (including ourselves) the necessity of their re/creation.

As a practical matter, this is what a daily walk in Christ looks like. Setting aside fantasies of gain or fears of loss, I sacrifice all things. I witness (and forgive) the sun's rising and setting. I witness (and forgive) the rain that falls and the heat that bakes. I witness (and forgive) the oatmeal that is cold and the fruit that has browned. I witness (and forgive) the pants that no longer fit. I witness (and forgive) my creaking knees and receding gums and graying beard. I witness (and forgive) the limits of my talents and success. I witness (and forgive) the independence of my children. I witness (and forgive) my wife's love. I witness (and forgive) the strengths and weaknesses of my parents. I witness (and forgive) the Church's still-in-progress embodiment of Christ. I witness (and forgive) the loss of all things. I witness (and forgive) the end of the world.

I witness (and forgive) the end of the world.

And forgiving all things—day by day, hour by hour, minute by minute—I stop defensively judging what the world deserves and finally find myself empowered, instead, to recognize what sacrifices this passing world needs.

Afterword

"How troubled is this world! It is born, it decays, and it dies. It falls away and then appears yet again."
—*The Buddha*

I wanted to write about Mormon because I've been thinking about the loss of all things. I've been thinking about the end of the world. And, especially, I've been thinking about climate change. While I'm a philosopher and not an expert in climate science, the broad outlines of the science aren't hard to follow and the most recent science is uniformly damning. Like the proverbial frogs in a pot, our water is starting to boil. The ecological deterioration, political upheavals, famines, water crises, energy shortages, and economic collapses we will predictably face on a global scale in the near future straightforwardly merit biblical language: we're looking at an apocalypse. The writing is on the wall. The baked and cracked remnant of a world that we will bequeath to our children and grandchildren will look nothing like the world we live in today.

This world is going to end.

Is this conclusion alarmist? Am I being hysterical? I fervently hope so.

As someone deeply conservative in bearing, I'm aware that there are good social, political, and (most pointedly) economic reasons to question whether we are witnessing the irreversible onset of catastrophic changes to the earth's climate. Unfortunately, there appear to be few, if any, *scientific* reasons to doubt the mountain of alarming evidence that the planet has reached a tipping point. I've seen convincing arguments, for instance, that even publicly discussing the coming cascade of climate tragedies is political suicide, a sure road to marginalization and political powerlessness. And I've also seen convincing arguments that trying to wean the global economy off its addiction to fossil fuels could itself catalyze the kind of economic implosion that an intervention was, at least in part, intended to avoid. But at a certain point—and at a certain point in the very near future—these political and economic arguments, however convincing, won't matter. At a certain point, the melting ice caps, rising sea levels, acidified oceans, droughts, wildfires, hurricanes, deforested lands, depleted soils, extreme weather, energy shortages, and mass extinctions of entire ecological networks will carry the day. And when that day comes, the patently sensible counterarguments we collectively raised as bulwarks against the brute *physics* of climate science won't matter much more than the paper they were printed on. Physics will carry the day.

What, in the face of this apocalypse, are we to do? Living through the end of the world, how should we, as disciples, respond?

For disciples of Christ, there is only one kind of work. We must, with clear eyes, have the courage to witness the end of the world. We must, rather than abusing the law to judge what is deserved, fulfill the law by judging what is needed. We must lay down our weapons, give up on revenge, and forgive the world's passing. We must sacrifice all things.

> Our choice is a clear one. We can continue acting as if tomorrow will be just like yesterday, growing less and less prepared for each new disaster as it comes, and more and more desperate-

ly invested in a life we can't sustain. Or we can learn to see each day as the death of what comes before, freeing ourselves to deal with whatever problems the present offers without attachment or fear. If we want to live in the Anthropocene, we must first learn how to die.[1]

The choice is clear. There are only two options: we can lose all things or we can sacrifice all things. Pretending that the world isn't going to end—pretending that these aren't the latter days—will only seal and intensify our loss.

What if, ultimately, the world doesn't end as predicted by climate science? What if the planet is hit by a comet instead? Or suffers nuclear annihilation? Or what if we develop a miracle technology that simultaneously sequesters our carbon, generates boundless energy, and painlessly alchemizes our global economy into something equitable and sustainable? What if, in the end, we all die peacefully in our sleep at the age of ninety-five?

If so, have we been spared?

Have we avoided the loss of all things?

While this scenario would be vastly preferable, nothing fundamental will have changed. Time—and God's endless work of re/creating the world—will remain implacable. We must still, with clear eyes, have the courage to witness the end of the world. We must still, with broken hearts, forgive the world its passing. We must still lay down our weapons, give up on revenge, and fulfill the law by judging what is needed. We must still sacrifice all things.

Our collective refusal to witness the coming climate catastrophe is the predictable effect of our collective refusal to sacrifice all things—or, often enough, any things.

Can we, like Mormon, still learn to care for a world that, on one scale or another, we are powerless to save? I've lost all hope that anything but the decisively Christian work of consecration could usher us (and our children, and our grandchildren) through the coming troubles that will cripple our world. I've lost all hope in anything but Christ.

God help us to take up this redemptive work in earnest.

God help us to take up this sacrificial work before the day of grace is past.

Further Reading

Damasio, Antonio. *Looking for Spinoza: Joy, Sorrow, and the Feeling Brain.* (New York: Houghton Mifflin Harcourt, 2003.)

Gardner, Brant. *Second Witness: Analytical and Contextual Commentary on the Book of Mormon, Fourth Nephi–Moroni.* (Salt Lake City, UT: Greg Kofford Books, 2007.)

Hardy, Grant. *Understanding the Book of Mormon: A Reader's Guide.* (New York: Oxford University Press, 2010.)

Hickman, Jared. "The Book of Mormon as Amerindian Apocalypse." *American Literature 86*, no. 3 (2014): 429–61.

Holland, Jeffrey R. "Mormon: The Man and the Book." *In The Book of Mormon: It Begins with a Family*, (Salt Lake City, UT: Deseret Book, 1983.) 214–29.

Miner, Alan C. "A Chronological Setting for the Epistles of Mormon to Moroni." *Journal of Book of Mormon Studies 3*, no. 2 (Provo, UT: Foundation for Ancient Research and Mormon Studies, 1994): 94–113.

Scranton, Roy. *Learning to Die in the Anthropocene: Reflections on the End of a Civilization.* (San Francisco: City Lights, 2015.)

Sorenson, John L. "Mormon's Sources." *Journal of the Book of Mormon and Other Restoration Scripture* 20, no. 2, (Provo, UT: Neal A. Maxwell Institute for Religious Scholarship, 2011): 2–15.

Wallace-Wells, David. *The Uninhabitable Earth: Life After Warming.* (New York: Tim Duggan Books, 2019.)

Wendt, Candice. "Mormon's Question." *Journal of Book of Mormon Studies 24* (Provo, UT: Neal A. Maxwell Institute for Religious Scholarship, 2015): 248–53

Endnotes

SERIES INTRODUCTION

1. Elder Neal A. Maxwell, "The Children of Christ," university devotional, Brigham Young University, Provo, UT, 4 February 1990, https://speeches.byu.edu/talks/neal-a-maxwell_children-christ/.

2. Elder Neal A. Maxwell, "The Inexhaustible Gospel," university devotional, Brigham Young University, Provo, UT, 18 August 1992, https://speeches.byu.edu/talks/neal-a-maxwell/inexhaustible-gospel/.

3. Elder Neal A. Maxwell, "The Book of Mormon: A Great Answer to 'The Great Question,'" address, Book of Mormon Symposium, Brigham Young University, Provo, UT, 10 October 1986, reprinted in *The Voice of My Servants: Apostolic Messages on Teaching, Learning, and Scripture,* ed. Scott C. Esplin and Richard Neitzel Holzapfel (Provo, UT: Religious Studies Center, Brigham Young University; Salt Lake City: Deseret Book, 2010), 221–38, https://rsc.byu.edu/archived/voice-my-servants/book-mormon-great-answer-great-question.

INTRODUCTION

1. Hugh Nibley, *Mormonism and Early Christianity*, ed. Todd M. Compton and Stephen D. Ricks (Salt Lake City, UT: Deseret Book, 1987): 303–304.

2. "History, 1838–1856, volume E-1 [1 July 1843–30 April 1844]," p. 1974, *The Joseph Smith Papers*, https://www.josephsmithpapers.org/paper-summary/history-1838-1856-volume-e-1-1-july-1843-30-april-1844/346

1

1. Ralph Waldo Emerson, "An Address delivered before the Senior Class in Divinity College, Cambridge," July 15, 1838.

4

1. For a crash course in the neurological importance of moods and emotions, try Antonio Damasio's *Looking for Spinoza: Joy, Sorrow, and the Feeling Brain* (New York: Houghton Mifflin Harcourt, 2003).

AFTERWORD

1. Roy Scranton, *Learning to Die in the Anthropocene: Reflections on the End of a Civilization*, (San Francisco: City Lights Publishers, 2015): 27.

Editions of the
Book of Mormon

Most Latter-day Saints are familiar principally with the official edition of the Book of Mormon published in 2013 by The Church of Jesus Christ of Latter-day Saints. It contains the canonical text of the book, divided into chapters of relatively even length with numbered verses for ease of access. Its footnotes aim to assist readers in seeking doctrinal understanding.

Other Book of Mormon editions are available and often helpful. Among these are official editions from earlier in the scripture's publishing history, which are relatively accessible. There are also editions published recently by a variety of presses meant to make the text more readable. Both types of editions are referred to throughout *Book of Mormon: brief theological introductions*. Also of importance (and occasionally referred to) are the manuscript sources for the printed editions of the Book of Mormon.

manuscript sources

Unfortunately, the original manuscript of the Book of Mormon was damaged during the nineteenth century, but substantial portions of it remain. All known extant portions have been published in typescript in Royal Skousen, ed., *The Original Manuscript of the Book of Mormon: Typographical Facsimile of the Extant Text* (Provo, UT: FARMS, 2001). A future volume of the Joseph Smith Papers will publish images of the extant manuscript, along with a typescript.

After completing the original manuscript's dictation, Joseph Smith assigned Oliver Cowdery to produce a second manuscript copy of the text. That manuscript has been called the printer's manuscript since it was designed for use by the first printer of the Book of Mormon. The printer's manuscript, which is more or less entirely intact, also contains corrections and other editorial markings inserted when the second (1837) edition of the Book of Mormon was being prepared. A typescript of the printer's manuscript can be found in Royal Skousen, ed., *The Printer's Manuscript of the Book of Mormon: Typographical Facsimile of the Entire Text in Two Parts,* 2 vols. (Provo, UT: FARMS, 2001). Full color images of the manuscript were subsequently published along with a transcript in the Joseph Smith Papers series: Royal Skousen and Robin Scott Jensen, eds., *Printer's Manuscript of the Book of Mormon*, 2 vols., vol. 3 of the *Revelations and Translations* series of The Joseph Smith Papers, ed. Dean C. Jessee, Ronald K. Esplin, and Richard Lyman Bushman (Salt Lake City: Church Historian's Press, 2015). The images and transcript of the printer's manuscript are also available at the Joseph Smith Papers website (www.josephsmithpapers.org/the-papers/revelations-and-translations/jsppr3).

historical editions

Multiple editions of the Book of Mormon were published during the lifetime of Joseph Smith. The first edition, published in Palmyra, New York, in 1830, appeared without versification and with fewer chapter divisions than the present canonical text. The text of the 1830 edition is available electronically at the Joseph Smith Papers website (www.josephsmithpapers.org/the-papers/revelations-and-translations/jsppr4) and in print through various publishers as a replica edition. The 1830 text is also available in Robert A. Rees and Eugene England, eds., *The Reader's Book of Mormon* (Salt Lake City: Signature Books, 2008), which is divided into seven pocket-sized volumes (each with an introduction by a scholar).

Joseph Smith introduced numerous minor changes into the text of the Book of Mormon when it was prepared for a second edition in 1837. Many of these changes are marked in the printer's manuscript. Most were aimed at correcting grammatical issues, but some, in a small handful of cases, were also aimed at clarifying the meaning of the text or its doctrinal implications. The 1837 edition is available electronically at the Joseph Smith Papers website (www.josephsmithpapers.org/the-papers/revelations-and-translations/jsppr4).

A third edition was prepared under Joseph Smith's direction in 1840, and evidence makes clear that the original manuscript was consulted carefully in preparing this edition. Some important errors in the earlier editions were corrected, further grammatical improvements were introduced, and a few other changes were made to the text for purposes of clarification. The 1840 edition can be read at the Joseph Smith Papers website (www.josephsmithpapers.org/the-papers/revelations-and-translations/jsppr4). It forms the basis for at least one printed edition as well: *The Book of Mormon*, trans. Joseph Smith Jr. (New York: Penguin Books, 2008), which contains

THE

BOOK OF MORMON:

AN ACCOUNT WRITTEN BY THE HAND OF MOR-
MON, UPON PLATES TAKEN FROM
THE PLATES OF NEPHI.

Wherefore it is an abridgment of the Record of the People of Nephi; and also of
the Lamanites; written to the Lamanites, which are a remnant of the House of
Israel; and also to Jew and Gentile; written by way of commandment, and also
by the spirit of Prophesy and of Revelation. Written, and sealed up, and hid
up unto the LORD, that they might not be destroyed; to come forth by the gift
and power of GOD unto the interpretation thereof; sealed by the hand of Moroni, and hid up unto the LORD, to come forth in due time by the way of Gentile;
the interpretation thereof by the gift of GOD; an abridgment taken from the
Book of Ether.

Also, which is a Record of the People of Jared, which were scattered at the time
the LORD confounded the language of the people when they were building a
tower to get to Heaven: which is to shew unto the remnant of the House of
Israel how great things the LORD hath done for their fathers; and that they may
know the covenants of the LORD, that they are not cast off forever; and also to
the convincing of the Jew and Gentile that JESUS is the CHRIST, the ETERNAL
GOD, manifesting Himself unto all nations. And now if there be fault, it he the
mistake of men; wherefore condemn not the things of GOD, that ye may be
found spotless at the judgment seat of CHRIST.

BY JOSEPH SMITH, JUNIOR,
AUTHOR AND PROPRIETOR.

PALMYRA:
PRINTED BY E. B. GRANDIN, FOR THE AUTHOR.

1830.

FIGURE 8   The title page of the original 1830 edition of
The Book of Mormon. © Intellectual Reserve, Inc.

a helpful introduction by Laurie Maffly-Kipp, a scholar of American religious history.

One other edition of the Book of Mormon appeared during the lifetime of Joseph Smith—an 1841 British edition, which was largely based on the 1837 edition and therefore lacked corrections and other improvements that appear in the 1840 edition. It, too, is available electronically at the Joseph Smith Papers website (www.josephsmithpapers.org/the-papers/revelations-and-translations/jsppr4).

In 1879, Latter-day Saint apostle Orson Pratt completed one of the more influential editions of the Book of Mormon published after Joseph Smith's death. Pratt lamented that too many Latter-day Saints left the scripture unread on the shelf. He sought to create an easier reading experience by dividing up the originally long chapters and adding verse numbers—revisions which have largely remained unchanged in the Church's official edition to the present. He also pioneered a system of cross-references and other explanatory footnotes. Most of Pratt's notes were removed or replaced in subsequent official editions—most thoroughly in the Church's 1981 edition when new descriptive chapter headings were introduced. These headings can still be found, with a few minor updates, in the 2013 edition.

A detailed and helpful devotional treatment of the publication history of the Book of Mormon can be found in Richard E. Turley, Jr. and William W. Slaughter, *How We Got the Book of Mormon* (Salt Lake City: Deseret Book, 2011). These authors trace developments in the format and study apparatuses used to present the text of the Book of Mormon to audiences from the 1850s to the present.

study and reading editions

The most important scholarly editions of the Book of Mormon are Grant Hardy, ed., *The Book of Mormon: A Reader's Edition* (Urbana and Chicago: University of Illinois Press, 2003); and Royal Skousen, ed., *The Book of Mormon: The Earliest Text* (New Haven, CT: Yale University Press, 2009).

Hardy's edition repackages the text of the 1921 public domain edition of the Book of Mormon. It contains a helpful introduction, a series of useful appendices, and a straightforward presentation of the text in a highly readable format. Footnotes are minimal—they are used only to clarify direct references or allusions within the text, to track dates, or to alert readers about original chapter divisions. This edition contains modern chapter and verse divisions, but they are unobtrusively typeset. The text is presented in straightforward paragraphs, with one-line headings marking text divisions. Poetry is set off in poetic lines, as in modern editions of the Bible.

Skousen's edition is the result of his quarter-century-long work with the manuscript and printed sources for the Book of Mormon text. The edition aims to reproduce as closely as can be reconstructed the words originally dictated by Joseph Smith to his scribes. Chapter and verse divisions familiar from recent editions are in the text (and symbols mark original chapter breaks), but the text is presented in what Skousen calls "sense lines"—each line containing (on Skousen's reconstruction) approximately what the prophet would have dictated at one time before pausing to allow his scribe to write. The edition contains helpful introductory material and a summary appendix noting significant differences between *The Earliest Text* and the current official edition. It is otherwise without any apparatus for the reader.

The most significant edition of the Book of Mormon deliberately constructed for a lay reading audience is Grant Hardy, ed., *The Book of Mormon: Another Testament of Jesus Christ, Maxwell Institute Study Edition* (Salt Lake City and Provo, UT: Neal A. Maxwell Institute, Deseret Book, and BYU Religious Studies Center, 2018). In this edition, Hardy uses the text of the 2013 official edition of the Book of Mormon but presents it in a readable way for everyday students of the volume. This edition reproduces the best of what appears in Hardy's *Reader's Edition* but adds further resources in the introductory and appendix materials. The footnotes are updated and expanded to include variant readings from the original and printer's manuscripts, and to provide notes about other textual details. The body of the text is presented, as in the *Reader's Edition*, in a straightforward fashion, readable and interrupted only by one-line headings. Modern chapter and verse divisions, as well as original chapter divisions, are easily visible.

Index

140

Colophon

The text of the book is typeset in Arnhem,
Fred Smeijer's 21st-century-take on late
18th-century Enlightenment-era letterforms
known for their sturdy legibility and clarity
of form. Captions and figures are typset in
Quaadraat Sans, also by Fred Smeijers.
The book title and chapter titles are typeset
in Thema by Nikola Djurek.

Printed on Domtar Lynx 74 gsm,
Forest Stewardship Council (FSC) Certified.

Printed by Brigham Young University Print & Mail Services

Woodcut illuminations Brian Kershisnik
Illumination consultation Faith Heard

Book design & typography Douglas Thomas
Production typesetting Maria Camargo

Mormon 1:2–4 . . . and I began to be learned
somewhat after the manner of the learning of
my people and Ammaron said unto me: I perceive that thou art a sober child, and art quick
to observe . . . and ye shall engrave on the plates
of Nephi all the things that ye have observed
concerning this people.